Get in Gear

Get in Gear
The Seven Gears that Drive Strategy to Results

Sean T. Ryan

Routledge
Taylor & Francis Group
A PRODUCTIVITY PRESS BOOK

First published 2020
by Routledge
52 Vanderbilt Avenue, New York, NY 10017

and by Routledge
2 Park Square, Milton Park, Abingdon, Oxon, OX14 4RN

Routledge is an imprint of the Taylor & Francis Group, an informa business

© 2020 Sean T. Ryan

Library of Congress Cataloging-in-Publication Data
Names: Ryan, Sean T., author.
Title: Get in gear : the seven gears that drive strategy to results / Sean T. Ryan.
Description: New York, NY : Routledge, 2020. | Includes bibliographical references and index.
Identifiers: LCCN 2020002274 (print) | LCCN 2020002275 (ebook) |
ISBN 9780367472955 (hbk) | ISBN 9780367471491 (pbk) | ISBN 9781003034742 (ebk)
Subjects: LCSH: Strategic planning. | Business planning. | Organizational learning. | Leadership.
Classification: LCC HD30.28 .R929 2020 (print) | LCC HD30.28 (ebook) |
DDC 658.4/012—dc23
LC record available at https://lccn.loc.gov/2020002274
LC ebook record available at https://lccn.loc.gov/2020002275

ISBN: 978-0-367-47295-5 (hbk)
ISBN: 978-0-367-47149-1 (pbk)
ISBN: 978-1-003-03474-2 (ebk)

Typeset in Minion
by codeMantra

Contents

Foreword

Some of you have probably experienced a point in your career when your candor and honesty are no longer appreciated in your organization. I had reached that point at Perrier Group of America when I met Sean Ryan.

It was the mid-1990s, and our CEO brought Sean in as a consultant to help spark a turnaround at our organization. I was a regional training director at Perrier and was instantly impressed with Sean and his ideas. He had an absolute belief in the work and in people's ability to do the work.

Many of Sean's ideas at the time would evolve into the Strategy-Execution-Results (SXR) process that you will read about in this book. The upshot is we were targeting work that would result in the organization's communicating better, having a consistent understanding of the company's goals and transforming from working as individuals to working as a team.

When Sean was recruiting a handful of employees for his team, to the surprise of the company's top executives, he asked me to join him. My habit of saying uncomfortable truths out loud, which they considered at best a mixed blessing, was exactly what Sean prized.

Working with Sean was unlike anything I had done before. We built organization development programs such as Service Quality Assessments, Leadership Forums, 360° Feedback Loops, and Performance Development Process during my four-plus years with him, much of the work was informed by the thousands of internal interviews we did across all levels and functions of the company. This 360° perspective allowed us to help Perrier leaders develop a deep understanding of their culture, values, and goals and how widespread they were shared throughout the organization and then build solutions that leadership could leverage to move the organization forward.

I eventually moved on to lead several organizations, but I can honestly say that a huge amount of what I know about how to lead and run a company I learned in the years I worked with Sean.

In my career, I've worked with countless people brought in from the outside to swoop in, diagnose what's ailing us, and solve the problem.

Sean stands out because even though he's there to teach, he's always listening and watching to see what teams and individuals can teach him.

I can't tell you how many times we would be in the middle of a multi-hour group exercise that had a specific objective – when someone would make a comment that Sean recognized as critical. He was fearless with these, willing to take the group on a detour, exploring what was behind that comment, and, more often than not, leading to the discovery of a hidden truth.

Maybe it was a tension between two people that was affecting everyone else, and nobody was willing to say anything about it. Maybe it was a clue that there was a disconnect between the company's intended culture and its real one. These detours were unplanned gems, and they often ended up being the most impactful part of Sean's work.

You don't capture those moments unless you have the quiet confidence to let the people you're leading steer the ship at times, trusting that they have the knowledge and motivation to solve their problems once you help them see what they're up against and the tools at their disposal. That's Sean's approach. He is fully aware of the many, many ways people can screw up, yet he's also the most optimistic person I know.

It's hardly surprising, but Sean proved to be a very patient and thorough teacher. When I joined his team, I didn't have a lot of experience with this kind of work. But he had what I would call highly misplaced but motivating confidence that I could do it. He had a calming and energizing presence. In his dealings with his team, Perrier executives, and the entire organization, he emphasized how to think, not what to think.

He was the first person I worked with who didn't just handle my questions. He *embraced* my questions. Sometimes, he'd respond, "That's a great question. Why don't you try to find an answer," which would launch me on a rewarding mini-journey.

Eventually, I left Perrier for a position at Aftermarket Technology Corporation, which put me on a path, after two mergers, to lead Fedex Supply Chain. Sean remained a valuable adviser and partner in my work over the next 20 years.

When our company, which had become GENCO, was merging into Fedex, I asked Sean to help us through the critical transition. On the one hand, we needed to preserve some of the GENCO culture, to assure our teammates that a part of the company they'd always known and loved would remain. On the other hand, we needed to integrate into Fedex's culture and methods, so the entire company could operate as a single team.

Fedex Supply Chain, which was being created with the merger, had not yet developed a clear set of strategic priorities.

Sean was the perfect person to help us on our journey. We set up two multi-day meetings and began by having everyone list their top three-to-five priorities, a process Sean will introduce you to in this book. We honed our strategy, aligned around our critical priorities, built our business cases for resources and investments needed, and aligned our team around ownership of actions and results. We determined how we were going to execute the strategy and how we were going to measure it. The work was instrumental to a successful integration, a cultural transformation, and dynamic growth of the business.

Sean doesn't need big stage settings like the launch of Fedex Supply Chain to make an impact. One evening, when I was still at Perrier, Sean and I were having dinner, and we got to talking about what I might want to do next and the steps I'd need to take to get there. He took notes on the back of a napkin and gave it to me at the end of the meal. It's still the best career development plan I've ever received, and it informed my career decisions for the next several years. I think I may still have the napkin somewhere.

Throughout my time with Sean, it was clear that he had developed a detailed process for bringing about and supporting success with critical change processes in an organization. I was lucky to witness the evolution of that process into this book you're about to read. Over the years, some of the terms may have changed, and Sean has added and subtracted elements as part of his perpetual fine-tuning of the process. But looking back, I can see the heart of SXR in everything we worked on.

This book is the result of a man with a vision who eagerly challenges and refines his ideas in the real world over and over. The result is nothing short of a map to transform any organization, no matter its size or purpose. As Sean would say, it's not a script. There is no list of steps to follow and no magic bullet that one day creates a transformed organization like switching on a light. Instead, this book presents you with a set of principles, guidelines written in English, not consultant-speak, and packed with examples from the hundreds of organizations' journeys that Sean has led. If you take the principles to heart, follow the guidelines and do the work, you will succeed. Just as he did a quarter century ago for me at Perrier, he won't teach you what to think or do. He'll teach you how.

Art Smuck, CEO (retired), FedEx Supply Chain

Acknowledgments

Heather, my wonderful spouse and best friend, who supported the crazy idea that I should write a book. Well, at least she didn't laugh hysterically at the thought! Your unending love and support make the journey worthwhile.

My kids, Aidan, Ashlee, and Kellen – my DNA is in you, but your DNA is all over this book. What I've observed, learned, and taught to individuals and organizations manifested itself in your daily experiences. I certainly learned from you and I hope you picked up a few things from dad along the way.

Mom and Dad – may you both be resting in peace. Dad, your humble, quiet leadership should serve as a model for dads and leaders everywhere. Growing up, I often asked my mom how she knew so much. She always responded, "I read a lot." Somewhere along the line I figured out that was a good idea. She often lamented that she couldn't explain to her friends what I did for a living as a "consultant." Now, wherever you are, you can just tell them, "He's an author." Way easier to explain!

Literally all the people I have worked with over the years. I've learned more from you than I could have from a thousand PhD programs at the best universities. Although, some of that is attributable to the fact that the best schools probably wouldn't let me on campus! I learned from all of you – what you struggled with, what drove your successes, what frustrated the hell out of you, and what you found joy in. What I learned from you is woven throughout the fabric of this book.

In particular,

Miller Templeton – you took some nerdy Civil Engineering student at Georgia Tech under your wing and taught me that all this "people stuff" can actually be taught and learned. You've impacted thousands of people in the most positive manner possible.

Rick Tate – nearly 40 years later, in spite of my best efforts to catch up, you've still forgotten more about leadership and organizations than I'll ever know or remember. I will always treasure, and never forget, the hours we spent in your office combing over every leadership theory ever known or developed. Your passion and patience were boundless. (Well, patience was mostly boundless!)

Art Smuck – I was lucky to cross paths with you in my early days working with Perrier. And, later, I was luckier to recruit you to my team there. You continue to be one of the best natural-born leaders I've met while continuing to passionately grow your capabilities at every step along the way. Your combination of caring deeply about the people around you while simultaneously challenging them to be their best sets both a high bar and a great example for others to follow.

All my friends and the people I've had a chance to work with at Nucor. I've met and learned from hundreds of Nucor teammates. It's hard to narrow it down to just a few, but I'll try. I'm incredibly appreciative of the opportunities and support provided by Dan Krug, Amy Fisher, Josh Wall, Leon Topalian, MaryEmily Slate, Johnny Jacobs, and John Farris. You provided the opportunity to experiment on your organizations with the concepts in this book. Somehow, everyone survived!

All the people who touched this book and helped bring it to fruition. One by one, this incredible team came together without which this book would suck badly and would never have seen the light of day.

> Cliff Glickman – who ghostwrote portions and edited everything else. Our evening conversations forced me to think through the issues and were instrumental to bringing this book to life.
>
> Tracey Ross-Watmore – your contributions to this book were enormous. Without them, this book would simply not exist. You brought an intuitive feel about how to make the concepts resonate with readers that makes the book worth reading. The research you did at the drop of the hat was both astounding and vital. Cajoling Greg into being one of the crash test dummies, pilot-testing the concepts was critical to making sure SXR works in the real world. Finally, from early on, you were the biggest cheerleader and supporter of the idea that this book should come to life.
>
> Dawn Mena – THE EDITOR whose insightful, crisp, specific feedback made every aspect of this book better.
>
> Dawn Drew – you possess an incredible ability to translate my hand-scrawled, barely legible graphics into visuals that effectively communicate the point. PLUS your patience in working through dozens of edits and tweaks was incredible.

Lois Moore – beyond being a phenomenal mother to Heather and the best-ever Nana to Aidan, you may also be the most sharp-eyed proofreader ever. The amount of red ink you used in proofing the manuscript might best be measured in barrels! I felt a huge sense of success when 1 page in the 200-page manuscript had no proofing marks on it!

Linda MacIntyre – you single-handedly hold everything at WWICI together, which makes everything else possible.

All those who came before me who observed, studied, wrote, and spoke about how organizations work: MacGregor, Drucker, Argyris, Peters, Waterman, Blanchard, Senge, Patterson, Brinkerhoff, and literally hundreds of others. In many respects, this book is a great big printed hip-hop song that samples from, and hopefully adds to, that massive body of work about what enables organizations and individuals to perform their best.

To all the clients who have trusted me with pieces of their organization and enabled this crazy Don Quixotic mission – to build great organizations where people can contribute their best every day – to take flight. You allowed me into the inner sanctum to experiment and learn at your expense. I can only hope I've somehow repaid the trust you placed in me.

Author

Sean Ryan is a world-renowned business consultant, speaker, trainer, and executive coach. As the founder of Whitewater International Consulting, he has worked internationally with companies such as Disney, Nucor Steel, and FedEx.

As former Vice President of Learning and Organizational Development for Perrier Group of America, Sean and his team shaped the organizational culture, people systems, and processes, as well as leadership capacity. Their work helped enable a fivefold increase in sales over a seven-year period.

With more than two decades of industry experience, Sean is highly regarded for his ability to guide organizations through complex transformational change in what he describes as "a world of perpetual whitewater." He helps clients formulate winning strategies and then deliver outstanding results through platforms including SXR™ (Strategy→Execution→Results), used by start-ups to Fortune 500 clients.

Beyond the organizational impact, Sean is amazed and humbled by the opportunity he's been provided to learn from the organizations and the hundreds of leaders he's had the pleasure to work with.

When not traveling for business and speaking engagements, Sean lives with his family in New Brunswick, Canada, where he serves as taste tester for his spouse's catering business. He also provides transportation services for his son and his friends, and he boats, skis, and bikes when time and his knees allow.

Introduction: Good Plans, Poorly Executed

You just spent an ungodly amount of time and/or money to develop your new strategy. You've produced a brilliant document that captures the strategy perfectly. Now, take that document, throw it in your desk drawer, and never look at it again.

Nobody in his right mind would do that, right? But if the people in your organization, or on your team, don't understand the strategy and their role in executing it, what's the difference?

The core purpose of "Strategy" is to energize and align people in an organization to propel it forward and help it succeed. A successful strategy should both guide and enable people to execute effectively at every level.

Unfortunately, organizations far too often do a poor job of translating that energy into the results they want or expect. Seventy-five to ninety percent of organizations fall short of achieving the results they expect from their strategies.

THE HIGH COST OF POOR EXECUTION

Most of the time, that's due to poor execution of good strategy. The shortfall is costly. Organizations can improve results by as much as 50% by executing their strategies more effectively. In the worst cases, poor execution of good strategy creates a doom loop. By underperforming, the organizations don't generate the returns they need to reinvest in their customers' experience, products, their team, or technology. So, they ultimately fall farther and farther behind.

I witnessed this firsthand early in my consulting career. We had been engaged to deliver leadership training at a PC manufacturer in California during the burgeoning days of the PC market. This gave us interesting insights into their efforts to execute a strategy to capitalize on the opportunities in the marketplace.

At the time, the PC industry was still quite fragmented. Our client had the fourth or fifth highest market share and a legitimate chance to grow. Their strategy was decent: be at the cutting edge of PCs as new generations of chips were introduced at a very competitive price.

But the execution was not nearly as crisp as it needed to be. The product development team would commit to aggressive timelines to develop the next generation of products. Within that culture, it was required to commit to the timeline regardless of how aggressive or ridiculous it seemed. Products were either rushed to market before they were truly ready and/ or delivered late to the market. There was no learning or accountability for missing deadlines. The only sin was not making the commitment in the first place.

Being late to market caused customers to shop elsewhere or caused our client to take lower prices (and lower margins) when they subsequently made it to the market. Rushing inferior products to market drove up costs. It doesn't take an MBA from Harvard or Stanford to figure out that lower prices, higher costs, and poor customer experience = pending failure. They ultimately merged with another company due to this doom loop caused by poor execution of a good strategy.

My personal journey began a little earlier when I started my career at Pacific Gas and Electric (PG&E) in California. Regardless of what people think of PG&E today, what I experienced was a company going through a massive transformation to be more focused on customers. Employees were generally talented, caring, and committed to doing the right thing. Yet they were rarely fully aligned across the organization. In other words, it wasn't always clear what the "right thing" was.

Everywhere I turned, I found talented, motivated people who wanted to do their best for the customers and the company.

Yet, somehow, time after time, we were inefficient, bureaucratic, and disconnected from our customers. The top executives would come up with an idea, and by the time that idea filtered down to the frontline workers, it barely resembled the original concept. When front line workers had ideas, they somehow got distorted before they reached the managers who could do something about them. Or they never reached that level at all.

There had to be a better way. The search for that better way launched my Don Quixotic journey to help create great organizations in which people could perform at their best.

The journey has often taken on the form of "What problem are we trying to solve?" Or, more directly, "How do we help this organization better engage their employees in the effort to translate their strategy into the results they want?"

The answers emerged, project by project, issue by issue.

Why Can't You Do What I Want?

I was sitting next to a sales manager and across from a production manager. The larger group we were working with had been going at it for a while, and people were getting frustrated just enough to start speaking some hard truths.

Sales manager to the production manager: "Why can't you produce the stuff we can sell?"

Production manager to the sales manager: "Why can't you sell the stuff we can make?"

Why Are 45-Minute Waits a Bad Thing?

A company operated what are now called theme parks but used to be called amusement parks. And it did a great job. The leadership decided it was time to expand into hotels.

The hotels struggled. Customers loved the company's amusement parks but hated their hotels. We were asked to help find out why.

The "why" turned out to be straightforward. Amusement park customers and hotel customers have *very* different service expectations. An amusement park customer will wait in line for 45 minutes if the ride is good enough. An amusement park customer will overpay for a lousy hamburger, because the next ride will make her forget all about the meal. But if you make a hotel customer wait 45 minutes to check in, you'll never see that customer again.

That wasn't the big revelation though. The big revelation came as we were going over the 75-page report in a group meeting. The CEO made it through a few pages before saying, "This feels like an overdose of chemotherapy." He went from person to person in the group, asking if the other executives were aware of how bad things were going at the hotel. He got a lot of sheepish replies. Turned out, a lot of people knew, but no one was willing to give the CEO the bad news.

How Do We Change a Light Bulb in Less than Six Weeks?

A manufacturer of heavy transportation equipment was having a terrible time with the massive maintenance department of one of its divisions. More than 1,200 skilled tradespeople were working hard at their jobs, but it seemed the company couldn't complete even the simplest task in less than a month.

We suspected the problem lay in the department's organization. Each function reported to its own group – electricians, mechanics, etc. But almost any job required people from a variety of functions. Whoever was responsible for a particular job invariably had to wait for other groups to free up resources to support the job. Those groups, in turn, had to plug their own holes wherever they loaned out a person. So, it would take weeks for the job to get started.

We gathered a group of 70 people from across all functions. We broke them into smaller groups, handed each group some blank paper, and said, "Design an organization that works." After a few tries, the groups converged on groups organized by production line. They put the new organization into action and, almost overnight, they were able to cut response time way down on high-priority work: hours or days versus weeks or months.

When Do We Serve the Bread?

A resort was struggling. The guest experience was poor, and funds and morale were low. We interviewed the resort's food and beverage people, looking for fast, inexpensive answers. I gave an overview at the start of one focus group and asked for any questions before we got started. "I want to know only one thing," a cook virtually screamed at me and the rest of the group. "When do we serve the bread?"

What?

After a little follow-up discussion, it became clear what he was talking about. The resort operator had developed a thick binder that aimed to dictate the proper protocol for any situation. Depending on the situation, the servers had at least eight different options for the optimal time to serve the bread, e.g., with the salad, with the soup, when the customer asked for it, or when Venus aligned with Mars.

If serving bread was this complicated, you can imagine what everyone's day was like at this resort. Simplifying the protocols didn't solve everything, but it was a big step in the right direction.

Finally, the Big Question: How Do We Align Performance at Every Level of Our Organization to Our Strategy?

We couldn't help but notice:

- Almost nobody had goals. Team members couldn't tell us what they were working toward. This shouldn't come as any surprise. How many of us, in our personal lives, really spell out goals, identify what to do to accomplish them, and then stick to them? (Short answer: 3% or less)

  Then, in that small minority of companies where people *did* have goals, many of them based their goals on activities, rather than results. A lot of companies, for example, set goals for their salespeople along the lines of making X number of calls in a week or a month. Suppose every salesperson in the company completed that goal. What does that get you? (Short answer: Lots of action, results only by accident.)

- When we asked people how they were performing ... by far, the most common answer was, "Well, I don't really know, but I'm not getting in trouble so I must be doing okay."

- And we often observed that people are busy. Really.damn.busy! Dozens of people told us that they "feel like pinballs, just being hit from bumper to bumper." Or, "I go home every day exhausted but can't identify a single thing I accomplished." And, when we've asked people what percentage of time they spend working on their top three goals (or, more loosely, "priorities," since so few actually have goals!!), the most common answer is, "Not much."

- Then we get to the paradox of learning and accountability. In a weird twist, in the rush to create accountability for performance, organizations often fail to learn why performance has fallen short. We don't consider whether the goal was right to begin with; or if there were barriers that got in the way of effective performance; or if there are systems, structure, process, or even culture issues that limit performance. We just want to hold someone accountable for the results they were supposed to generate. (Forgetting that, in a lot of cases, people aren't even clear what those results are supposed to be!)

  Yet, when we ask people to describe what accountability looks like in their organization, the most common answer is, "The only thing consistent about accountability here is that there is no consistency to it!"

So, you get the anti-paradox: no learning and no accountability instead of getting BOTH learning and accountability!

Which brings us back to the original premise of the journey I started over 30 years ago: there has to be a better way to engage everyone in the organization and align them to the strategy. To create great places to work where everyone can contribute their best.

And, there is!

It's not impossible. It can be achieved.

The answers lie in the pages of this book.

1

The Strategy to Results Gap: Why Execution Matters

What the hell is going on out there?

Several years ago, we were working with the top 25 leaders of an organization that had been struggling for a while. We started simply: we asked the leaders to write down the company's top three priorities for resolving their issues and improving their results. Ideally, if the organization was truly aligned and driving its Strategy to Execution to Results, we would have ended up with one list of three. Instead, we got back 25 nearly unique lists, consisting of about 70 different "top priorities."

Is it any wonder that the organization was performing poorly? Twenty-five leaders each leading their part of the organization in 25 directions. It was like my golf game: one shot sliced into the trees; next shot duck-hooked into a pond. No chance of executing my golf game to a more consistent, aligned approach to get close to par. If Vince Lombardi had been coaching that leadership team, he might have been compelled to repeat his famous sideline question, "What the hell is going on out there?"

Tom Peters, one of the leading experts in organizational leadership, often talks about "getting the herd moving roughly west." The leadership team we worked with that day had a different approach: "get the herd moving in every direction." As a result, the herd ended up getting nowhere.

FIXING THE EXECUTION GAP

Why is the problem of executing strategy and delivering results so prevalent? A recent Google search of "executing strategy" returned over 45 million hits in 0.55 seconds. There seem to be thousands of books written on the subject, each with plenty of advice on executing strategy to deliver great results for your organization. At least one of them must have the answer, right? The key to unlock your company's potential?

With all this sage advice out there, why aren't we all succeeding, or at least, like the young population of Lake Wobegon, all above average? Because no one has solved the problem of the Execution Gap.

The Execution Gap is well documented

- *Fortune* Magazine: "Less than 10% of strategies, effectively formulated, are effectively executed."
- *Harvard Business Review*: "The prize for closing the strategy-to-performance gap is huge – an increase in performance of anywhere from 60% to 100% for most companies."
- *Fortune* Magazine: "You'd never guess it from reading the papers or talking to your broker or studying most business books, but what's true at Compaq is true at most companies where the CEO fails. In the majority of cases – we estimate 79% – the real problem isn't the high-concept boners the boffins love to talk about. It's bad execution. As simple as that: not getting things done, being indecisive, not delivering on commitments."

Why do so many organizations come up short in translating their strategy to real results? Sometimes, it's the strategy itself. Maybe it's an ill-conceived acquisition. Maybe the strategy is formulated without an understanding of how to actually create value for their intended audience. In those situations, it's a case of "bad plan, poorly executed."

But most of the time, it's not your strategy. The plans are well thought out. It's your execution that's – ahem – killing you. Converting strategy to results can be difficult. Some of those thousands of strategy books promise a near-miraculous transformation of your company – a revolution if you just follow the plan. But the plan feels like such a heavy lift that the urge to set it aside and get back to doing business on familiar terms becomes irresistible.

We have a friend who's been in pretty good shape most of his life. But work demands caused him to stop exercising and eating right. As a result, he gained 20–25 pounds. In a burst of inspiration one weekend, he decided that he was going to get back in shape by training to compete in a triathlon. His thinking was, "That's the motivation I need to get back on track." He lasted about three days. His body was in a lot of pain, and the gap he needed to close seemed infinitely wide. As much as we're big fans of stretch goals – see Chapter 5 – trying to solve the whole problem at once can get in the way of taking the fundamental actions, the day-to-day blocking and tackling, which you need to be successful.

You don't have to swing for the fences to translate strategy to results. You can get there with a series of manageable steps. Each step will make an impact on your performance, and you'll gradually get better. If you stick with it, you might find that as you get the hang of things, the steps get easier and the changes more impactful. And you very well might discover one day that your company has indeed transformed, almost by stealth.

Now, don't get me wrong. I'm all for upfront, revolutionary change. If you feel like your organization needs a complete overhaul from top to bottom, this book will show you how to get there, through what we call the Strategy Execution Results (SXR) Framework.

But you might have a more focused change in mind, at least for starters. Maybe your company must improve its on-time delivery or cost control. Or your organization needs an infusion of new team members with varied capabilities to execute your strategy. Or maybe you are ready to introduce your products and services to a different target market – and you need results right now. This book will give you a menu of options to get there. You can pick one or two and start today.

Let me point out another problem with all those other strategy books: They almost always focus on the CEO of a large organization. But what if you're a mid-level manager just trying to get her team of six people to perform better? What if you're on the frontline of the organization and just trying to do your job a little better? For that matter, maybe your goal is to lose weight or save extra money for retirement or that vacation you want to take next year. The assumption that you have an entire organization's resources and strategic direction under your control doesn't apply to you.

No matter what your position in the organization is, or the type of goal you have, the SXR Framework can guide you through change in whatever unit, division, or team you lead or just for yourself.

To put it in tech terms, the SXR Framework is scalable. You can change one three-member team or a Fortune 500 company with hundreds of global locations. You can fix a single customer service issue or radically transform how you compete. No matter how small or large your problem, the SXR Framework will guide you to a solution that works.

With that bold claim out of the way, let's take a step back and ask a simple question: Who survives and prospers?

DIGGING IN: MANEUVERING THROUGH THIS WORLD OF PERPETUAL WHITEWATER

Back in university, when I admittedly spent as much time paddling white-water rivers all over the Southeast as I did going to class, my friends and I would often paddle Section 4 of the Chattooga. Serious "expert only" whitewater. Yeah, cue the "Deliverance" Dueling Banjos music in the background. As tight and technical as that section of the Chattooga is, on most days, we paddled most of the rapids with no special preparations. But not Five Falls. Any one of the rapids in Five Falls would be legendary on its own. Taken together, they are fraught with danger and have been the scene of multiple deaths over the years.

That's why Five Falls always required that we "dig-in." We scouted ahead to make sure we knew the conditions and whether the debris was clogging up any of the usual routes through the rapids. We made sure to deploy people with safety ropes at the critical rescue points. We'd coach and counsel each other about the best passages. And then we all paddled like hell through each of them, helping each other, cheering everyone on, and rescuing swimmers and boats when necessary. When we finished Five Falls, we'd celebrate our individual and collective success both on the river and then, later, at the bar.

Many of the factors that drive success on a whitewater rafting adventure are the same factors that drive success in the business world. Organizations that prosper and sustain themselves in a climate of perpetual chaos (whitewater) share several common key factors. They

1. Chart a course (strategy) that allows them to not just survive, but thrive, in a constantly changing environment.
2. Build the organizational capabilities necessary to maneuver through the whitewater without capsizing.
3. Execute quickly and effectively to take advantage of the circumstances.
4. Adapt to the rapidly changing environment and evolve to a new strategy.

The one compelling difference: In the business world, there is no safety line. If we're not prepared, if we don't understand where we are and where we want to go, if we don't have the necessary leadership or take the time to develop the talent we need, failure is certain. No one is waiting at the bottom of the rapids with a throw rope to pull us out if we veer off course.

Many have described this world of perpetual whitewater with the acronym VUCA: Volatile, Uncertain, Complex, and Ambiguous. Those VUCA components make effective execution more difficult, but they also put a premium on people who can engage everyone in the organization to execute their strategy quickly and effectively. The competitive environment is so turbulent that if you don't execute your strategy quickly, you may have to change the strategy before the old one is fully implemented.

People use the word "strategy" in many different contexts. For the purposes of this book, we like Michael Porter's classic definition of strategy[1] as:

Establishing a unique sustainable, defensible competitive position for the company that customers value.
Aligning the activities of the organization to that strategy, recognizing that competitive advantage arises from the fit across activities.
Making clear trade-offs and choices versus the competition.

In today's VUCA environment, "sustainable" and "defensible" can be fleeting. Just when you think you have a positioning that works…

- Someone identifies customer choice factors that you missed and provides a product or service offering that customers value more than yours.
- Someone comes along with similar products and services at a lower cost.

---

[1] Michael Porter, "What is Strategy?" *Harvard Business Review*, November–December 1996.

- Someone finds a way to be easier to do business with, or…
- Someone like Amazon or Uber comes along and disrupts the whole industry.

Poof. There goes your advantage.

"Sustainable and defensible" might mean that you have weeks or months to execute your strategy, not years that you might have had in the past. Executing rapidly and effectively is critical to creating competitive advantage. Otherwise, your opportunity has vanished. And often it's difficult to catch up. Poor execution delivers poor results, which then limits potential capital that can be reinvested to evolve strategy, improve execution, and deliver better results.

Porter also said that strategy is about aligning the activities of the organization to the strategy and making choices about what you will and won't do. You don't have the resources to spend time and energy on stuff that doesn't matter. Yet in virtually every organization, people are spending time, energy, and resources on stuff that just doesn't matter to the execution of the organization's strategy. The SXR Framework helps you identify at every level of the organization the activities that contribute to the execution of the strategy – and those that don't.

MOVING BEYOND A STRATEGY OF "JUST SUCKING LESS"

You might be thinking, "Okay, our execution may not be great, but everyone else's sucks too. Maybe if we just don't suck as badly as they do, we'll be all right."

That's actually not a terrible game plan to start with. At some point, you'll need a better one, but if "sucking less" gets you started, that'll work. Ideally, you'd like a plan that can accommodate these first baby steps, then take you past them.

This is where the SXR Framework comes into play.

The SXR Framework shows you how to step up your game gradually, methodically, with the flexibility to adjust to a new competitor or an industry disruptor. If you're ready to excel today, even better!

Through our work over the last 30 years with hundreds of clients across multiple industries – from start-ups to Fortune 100 companies – we've identified 7 Gears of Execution (shown in Figure 1.1) that effectively connect Strategy to Execution to Results.

The seven gears fall into two categories:

Environment Gears create *organizational surroundings* that enable success.

1. Right, Right, Right: Getting the right people in the right roles with the right capabilities. The goal is an organization in which everyone is engaged and working in concert. Organizations must hire the talent they need to support the strategy. But, hiring talent isn't sufficient. They must also hire people who fit within the value set of the organization. Organizations must help people grow their capabilities over time to enable the organization to adapt to rapidly changing environments.

2. Align the Architecture: Ensuring the organization's systems, structures, processes, and culture all shape effort toward execution of the strategy. Aligned architecture creates organizational gravity, a sort of unseen force that pulls people in the right direction.

3. Culture of Communications: Ensuring communication up, down, and across the organization so that everyone has the most timely and accurate information to make decisions and take action. Leaders at every level are constantly talking with and *listening to* their employees. They see things from their employees' points of view.

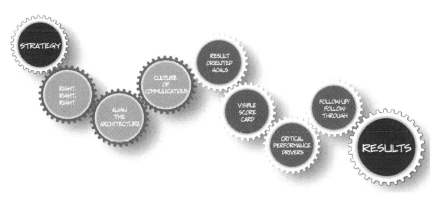

FIGURE 1.1 The SXR Framework: 7 Gears of Execution.

Performance Gears provide the *linkages* that connect Strategy to Execution to Results.

4. SET Result-Oriented Goals: Result-Oriented Goals ensure that everyone's efforts are aligned to executing the organization's strategy and delivering real accomplishments, not just generating activity. SET requires that goals have a Starting point, Ending point, and a Timeframe. This channels energy to the accomplishment of the goals.

5. Build Visible Scorecards: Visible Scorecards ensure everyone has the relevant, timely information they need to alter their performance to hit the goals *while the game is being played*. They help everyone own their results. A monthly sales report that comes out 10 days after the close of the month doesn't help salespeople take the necessary actions to hit this month's goals.

6. Identify the Performance Drivers: Performance Drivers are what people actually DO. They are tasks, behaviors, and activities that separate great from average performance.

7. Follow-up/Follow-through: Establish a process that generates learning and accountability for performance. Consistent Follow-up/Follow-through is the glue that holds the Seven Gear Framework together. It creates accountability for performance and living up to the organization's values. Just as important as accountability, Follow-up/Follow-through generates learning about where performance is on track and where and why it's off-track. It's the key to organizational learning and continuous improvement.

When the 7 Gears of Execution are actively managed together, they

- Align the organization to a common vision, strategy, and set of priorities.
- Set the foundation for effective execution.
- Drive execution of the competitive strategy throughout the organization.

To get an idea of how the 7 Gears of Execution work together, let's imagine you and a few friends want to lose weight together. To apply the SXR Framework, you might

- Start by making sure everyone in the group is motivated and supportive, weeding out anyone who isn't. You might add some outside resources to your support team – maybe a nutritionist or a personal trainer to provide guidance and accountability (Right, Right, Right).
- Invent ways for the group to meet and support each other – monthly lunch meetings, a "designated driver" who rides everybody for a month, a competition for most pounds lost over the summer (Align the Architecture).
- Create a Facebook page for everyone to contribute stories and a weekly catch-up phone call. Everyone would be engaged in providing each other the tough feedback they need to be successful (Culture of Communications).
- Have everyone report their current weight and the weight they plan to be in 90 days (SET Goals).
- Require weekly weigh-ins and post the results in a group email (Visible Scorecards).
- Set up weekend jogging groups and tennis dates to promote exercise and share articles on low-calorie meals (Identify Performance Drivers).
- Establish monthly check-ins where everyone reports his weight. Conduct meetings and phone calls to help anyone who falls behind (Follow-up/Follow-through).

WHY GEARS?

Gears transmit energy. The more aligned they are, and the less friction in the chain of gears, the better they function. The leader's job is to constantly align the gears so that people can contribute their best every day. Misalignment and friction make it difficult for the chain of gears to translate energy to results. The greater the misalignment, the less energy gets translated and the lower the performance of the organization.

The gears make it clear that *you don't have to fix everything all at once to improve the amount of energy translated to results.* The more alignment the better, but as a leader, you can identify the gears creating the most friction. That makes it easier to identify where you need to put your time, energy, and attention. This is what makes the step-by-step approach feasible. The seven gears are rarely fully aligned, but when they are, it's a thing of beauty!

Everyone in the organization has some control or influence over every gear. Nobody gets a hall pass. No one may say, "There's nothing I can do about that." There may be some gears you have more leverage over, or can act on more quickly, but you can have influence over every gear.

We're not saying that the SXR Seven Gear Framework will have your organization figuratively playing below par golf in every round or hitting dead center fairway with every shot you take. But improving the gears in most need of alignment will help you put a higher percentage of your shots in the fairway. Ultimately, the SXR Framework will help you deliver better results – even if that means "sucking less" – than not managing the gears at all.

GETTING STARTED: A CRISP, CLEAR, COMPELLING VISION/STRATEGIC INTENT

This book focuses on using the SXR Framework to drive the execution of your organization's strategy to better results. Before we get there, remember that execution requires strategic intent – what the organization is driving toward. We've seen dozens of highly optimized execution efforts that were completely disconnected from the organization's strategy – great execution, requiring much effort, yet completely wasted.

Execution must start with a compelling purpose or strategic intent. Team members need to know where you want to go. They can't execute something that they don't comprehend. When they understand your strategic intent and they have the responsibility and autonomy to act, they can get excited about moving the organization in that direction. They have something to align to.

While it may not be necessary for every team member to be able to recite the organization's strategy by heart, they DO need to understand the overall direction and their role in making that vision come alive.

You might think your organization has a great strategy, but unless your team members understand it and can outline their roles to help execute it, you don't actually have it! Remember our struggling organization at the start of this chapter.

By the same token, we've worked with dozens of organizations that thought they knew how they created unique value for their customers. But when we talked to the customers, we found that the companies didn't understand critical parts of the customers' point of view.

Here's a simple test to check whether your team understands your strategic intent:

- Can your team members give you a one- or two-sentence description of how your company distinguishes itself?
- Can they tell you the top two or three things the company must be great at, or must get better at, to be successful?
- Can they tell you how the previous two answers translate into the critical three to five things *they must accomplish* to contribute to the execution of the strategy?

If you can't answer those questions about your organization's strategy or you're a leader in the organization and your team can't answer those questions, it would be worth taking the time to get those answers. Then, your first assignment in translating Strategy to Execution to Results is to make sure you and everyone in your organization know the direction you're headed and their role in the effort to execute that strategy.

THOUGHT STARTER QUESTIONS

- How crisp and clear is your organization's strategy to the people who are responsible for executing it every day?
- How well can team members at every level of your organization describe their role in executing your strategy?
- How effectively are you translating Strategy to Execution to Results? Are you in the 10% that are generating the results you expect? Or are you in the other 90%?

FIRST STEPS

1. Evaluate your strategy from your customers' perspective. How does your perspective on what creates competitive advantage compare to what your customers think?
2. Find out from your team what they think your strategy is.
3. Find out how they think they connect their efforts to the strategy.
4. Find out what gets in the way of your organization being able to execute your strategy more effectively.

BIBLIOGRAPHY

Bossidy, Larry, Charan, Ram, & Burck, Charles. (2002). *Execution*. New York, NY: Crown Business.

Charan, Ram & Colvin, Geoffrey. (July 21, 1999). Why CEOs Fail It's Rarely for Lack of Smarts or Vision. Most Unsuccessful CEOs Stumble Because of One Simple, Fatal Shortcoming. *Fortune Magazine*.

HBO. (December 11, 2010). *Lombardi* NFL Films. https://www.hbo.com/sports/lombardi/index.html

Keillor, Garrrison. (July 1974). News from Lake Wobegon. A Prairie Home Companion. *American Public Media*.

Kiechel, Walker. (December 27, 1982). Corporate Strategists Under Fire. *Fortune Magazine*, P38.

Mankins, Michael & Steel, Richard. (July–August 2005). Turning Great Strategy into Great Performance. *Harvard Business Review*.

Peters, Tom & Austin, Nancy. (1986). *A Passion for Excellence*. New York, NY: Random House.

Porter, Michael E. (1980). *Competitive Strategy*. New York, NY: The Free Press.

Porter, Michael. (November–December 1996). What is Strategy? *Harvard Business Review*.

Volatility, Uncertainty, Complexity and Ambiguity [VUCA] Introduced by the US Army War College to describe the increasingly turbulent world in roughly 1987.

2

Right, Right, Right: The Right People with the Right Capabilities in the Right Roles

We worked with a Southern California division of a company that had clearly identified the overall business direction and values necessary to drive the business forward. Their previous sales and service function had been organized as a group of staunchly individual contributors driving sales within their individual territories. It became clear that this was eroding the customer experience and causing customers to leave the business. The new strategy, and aligned values, required a more customer service-oriented, team-based approach.

One team member, a strong informal group leader, resisted the change effort. He had a strong personality and was well-respected by the other 50 or so team members for the results he delivered under the previous strategy. However, he was an outspoken critic of the new strategy and the changes the organization was asking the team to make. Mostly, he resisted because he felt like he would be less successful (read: well-paid) executing the new strategy.

While many of the other team members felt the new strategy was the right way to go, and they could clearly see the reasons for it, they would not fully commit because of the vocal resistance of the group leader. For more than a year, that division's results limped along while other divisions within the company embraced and executed the new strategy. No amount of conversation by the division leaders could turn the one team member around. Finally, they decided to let him go. It was like flipping a light switch. Within a day or two all of the team members who had silently supported the change were fully engaged. Both the culture and the performance of the division turned around within days of the departure.

RIGHT PEOPLE IN THE RIGHT ROLES WITH THE RIGHT CAPABILITIES IS CRITICAL

Great strategy without the right people with the right capabilities is an illusion. You can have a compelling picture of where you want to go, but without the right people with the right capabilities, good luck getting there.

You never "solve" the Right, Right, Right issue. As competitive requirements change, the capabilities of team members at all levels of the organization must also adapt. And those people must have access to the resources they need to be successful. Organizations must provide access to growth and development opportunities they need to be successful. The best organizations continually address Right, Right, Right.

Organizations that are the most effective in translating strategy to execution make explicit decisions about the values that align with their strategy, and the capabilities and skills necessary to execute the strategy. Then they intentionally acquire and grow the talent they need to fuel their success.

Getting the Right People in the Right Roles with the Right Capabilities to drive your strategy to results involves four key elements:

- Know what you want.
  - Values-fit PLUS technical/functional capability PLUS ability to grow.
- Engage the people you have.
- Assess your talent and bench strength.
- Build capabilities: Development that works.

KNOW WHAT YOU WANT

Obviously Right, Right, Right means having the talent on your team to execute your strategy and deliver the results you want. Virtually everyone wants to hire people with the best technical/functional skills or most experience available. After all, if you're trying to design the next generation of smart phones, you want the best engineers on staff, right?

The problem with this kind of thinking is that it begins and ends with talent. Which candidate has the best technical skills? Who has the most experience? The company ignores the candidate's fit with their organization's values. The new person will learn that on the job, they figure. They figure wrong.

Values-Fit PLUS Technical/Functional Capability PLUS Ability to Grow

Getting people who fit the values of the organization is critical. Many organizations say they value integrity, respect, inclusion, and teamwork. But they continue to recruit, hire, tolerate, and even promote people who fall short in these areas because they "deliver results." They either neglect or don't realize the short-term/long-term trade-off that a poor values-fit very likely will disengage other team members and hurt those results over the long term.

Let's also be clear that defining the values critical to your organization and execution of your strategy goes well beyond merely stating what you value. Almost everyone SAYS they value integrity, respect, and inclusion. It would not go over well if the values statement said, "We value cut-throat, ill-tempered arsonists." But if that's who you hire, reward, promote, or even just tolerate, that's what you get.

When I joined Perrier Group of America, the organization consisted of multiple cultures spread across more than 80 locations in North America. The company had been created through the acquisition of a series of regional brands of bottled spring water. Each acquisition had their own cultures, and some had multiple cultures within the same operation.

- Some locations were more customer and service oriented; others were more "sales driven."
- Some were very command-and-control oriented; others delegated responsibility and latitude to act.
- Some locations had high levels of accountability and performance; others could be described as "the only thing consistent about the accountability was the inconsistency of it."

The organization didn't have a clear understanding of the values necessary to fuel its success or what is expected of leaders. Every location operated like its own little fiefdom.

At the time, companies like Pepsi and Coca-Cola had not yet entered the bottled water industry. But we knew that day was coming. With our disjointed culture and leadership practices, we were not ready to compete successfully against them. So, it was critical to define a set of values – which we ultimately labeled "Our Beliefs" – to shape the culture we wanted to create.

The essential questions were the following:

- What do we stand for?
- What do we believe in?
- What are the broad boundaries we want people to play within that enable us to execute our strategy?

We collected input from hundreds of people at all levels of the organization, and then whittled them back to these common themes that aligned with our strategy:

- Respect for people, community, and the environment.
- Honesty and integrity.
- Teamwork.

Ultimately, we wove these beliefs into everything we did. See Chapter 3: Align the Architecture for why this is so critically important. These beliefs shaped who we hired, who was promoted, and, in some cases, who left. They were also embedded in our training and development efforts, especially new team member orientation and leadership development programs.

The change was not instantaneous, but over a relatively short period of time (one to two years, not the five to seven years that many organizational theorists suggest it will take), the culture evolved to align more closely with our espoused values. We generated a virtuous cycle: As our culture aligned with our values and our strategy, we were able to attract more of the people who fit our value set, and more people in the organization became more aligned with both the strategy and the values.

Defining Values: The Non-Negotiables

Over the years, we've identified three values that are essential throughout all industries and companies:

1. Integrity.
2. Respect.
3. Trust.

Those three values are critical for unleashing the commitment, passion, and energy of everyone on the team. People want to work in environments in which people honor their commitments, they can trust those around them, and they are respected for everything they bring to the table. When organizations talk about diversity and inclusion, aren't they really talking about respect?

These foundational values are crucial to creating an environment that allows organizations to fully translate strategy to results. A few examples we'll explore in this book:

Aligning the Architecture – which we explore in Chapter 3 – involves changes to an organization's systems, structures, and processes to best align them to the strategy. Those changes are difficult under the best circumstances. Team members always wonder, "What's going to happen to me? How will I be impacted?" If the underlying value-set is strong – "I know you are honest, and you trust and respect me" – it's easier to change reporting structures, work processes, or even compensation. If it's weak, people want to cling to the safety of what they know.

In Chapter 4, we explore how vital Communications are to driving strategy to execution to results. Having a solid foundation of honesty and respect is crucial for information to flow quickly and accurately up, down, and sideways through the organization to ensure everyone has the information they need to perform their best. For instance, bad news should travel as quickly as good news. But if I'm afraid of what you'll do with the bad news, the speed of information slows dramatically and, in the worst cases, grinds to a halt.

Later in this chapter, we discuss delegating responsibility and latitude to team members to execute the strategy. That invariably involves some failure as team members learn through experience. But the willingness to experiment, innovate, or improve declines dramatically when people fear that leaders will punish them for their inevitable mistakes.

Other values like teamwork or innovation will often be a function of the specific business strategy of the organization involved. A company exploiting a fast-growing technology, for example, likely would place a premium on adding innovative risk-takers to its team. A not-for-profit with a staff of four might favor people with a very flexible view of their job descriptions.

The critical issue is to be clear up front about what values your organization needs to support the execution of your strategy. If "teamwork" is vital to success, and you hire and promote independent go-getters, you'll likely find yourself frustrated when those people don't play well together. They, in turn, will be frustrated by your efforts to get them to work well with others, instead of letting them loose.

ENGAGE THE PEOPLE YOU HAVE

Recruiting the right people is only the start.

You also have to fully engage them in the journey if you want to be as successful as you can be.

Over the years, we've seen dozens of organizations attract great people who seemed like a great fit, only to watch them leave the organization within a short period of time because the organization was not effectively engaging them and utilizing their talents.

Based on our research and experiences, we've found that engaging environments share these characteristics:

Define the Playing Field

People always want to know:

- How to play the game, and
- How to win.

Think about inviting a friend who has never played poker to a game night at your house. Where would you start? You'd probably explain the pecking order of different poker hands, how a full house beats a flush, which beats a straight, etc. Then you might walk him through how the cards are dealt in say, Texas Hold 'Em, when everybody bets, and the options to call or raise. As you're explaining how to play, you'll probably include some house rules: maximum and minimum bets, ante amounts, the night's winner buys the food next time, etc. You might even play a couple of practice hands before you start playing to make sure they understand the game well enough to stay engaged in it.

A few years ago, my kids taught me the value of "Defining the Playing Field." They were playing a pick-up soccer game with their neighborhood friends. After a minute or two, someone kicked the ball up the street: GOAL! The team celebrated. The other team said it wasn't a goal. They argued for a while and started again. The ball went into the bushes. Out of bounds, one side said. No, it's not, said the other.

The kids wound up spending more time arguing than playing, and everyone soon just gave up and quit. Even in a pick-up, neighborhood soccer game, nobody wants to play if they don't know the rules.

There are two critical components of Defining the Playing Field within organizations: A **Clear and Compelling Purpose** – which defines how we WIN the game – and a **Shared Value Set** – which outlines the broadest set of rules about HOW we play the game.

Rally Everyone Behind a Clear, Compelling Purpose

People want to contribute to something that matters. They want to feel that they are doing something important, something bigger than themselves. Look at the success of companies such as TOMS® shoes and its pledge to give shoes and other essentials (such as sight, water, safe birth, and bullying prevention services) to match its customers' purchases.

Every great organization that fully engages its employees has a cause worth committing to. It doesn't have to be an external cause. Your organization's success might be all your team needs to stay motivated.

Promote a Widely Shared Value Set

Shared values essentially outline the "rules" by which people play in your organization. They are the widest parameters of acceptable behavior. The values, as we outlined above, must be intimately intertwined with your purpose and strategy. Your values describe WHO you aspire to be. They should drive your culture. Your culture describes who you actually ARE – how people actually behave. There is always a gap between the values and the actual culture. No one is perfect all the time. But wide gaps quickly put the lie to the values. And people in the organization can sense that gap from a mile away. It's critical to consistently reinforce the values so that people know what behavior is in bounds and what behavior is out of bounds.

Give Everyone a Significant Role in the Show

People want to contribute to the organization's success. If they feel boxed in, held back, or like they're not essential, they'll either tune out or move on.

Love 'em, or hate 'em, the Alabama Crimson Tide football program is a fantastic example of making everyone associated with the program feel like they have a significant role in the show. Some are obvious:

> The coaches recruit, develop, and coach up the best talent available. (Often using Strategy-Execution-Results (SXR) principles, by the way.)
> The players keep fit, eat healthy, stay in school, practice and execute the game plan.
> The training staff keeps the players healthy.

Some roles are a little less obvious:

> The alumni support recruiting and provide money to ensure the team has the best coaching talent and the best facilities, which enables both recruiting and player development.
> The fans provide the excitement, the support, and the screaming to fire up the players. They're definitely well trained. When Alabama is driving, what do the fans do? They get quiet so the team can hear the quarterback's signals. When the visitors are driving, the 'Bama fans get LOUD. They know their role: disrupt the other team's offense as much as possible – because they are committed to the cause: Help Alabama win its next National Championship.

From the receptionist at the front desk to the people on the loading dock, and all the way to the CEO, people want to feel like what they do matters to the success of the organization and its mission and purpose. Sadly, in so many organizations, no one ever helps connect the dots.

You have to know your team and what drives them. What gets them fired up about working for you and your company? What turns them off? What gets in their way?

A "Significant Role in the Show" means that every team member must have responsibility and latitude to act.

Your people can't have a significant role in the show if they don't have the responsibility and latitude to make decisions. Some organizations are heavy on the responsibility ("It's your fault we lost that client") but light on the latitude ("Follow the sales script on every call"). Giving both means letting your people make mistakes and learn from them.

Provide the Tools and Resources for People to Perform Their Best

All the responsibility and latitude in the world won't help if your people are using outdated technology or inferior equipment compared to their counterparts at your competitors.

In addition to physical products, tools and resources also include:

- Training and development opportunities that support job performance.
- Education and implementation of new skills and capabilities as technology and job requirements evolve.
- Sharing the information and feedback people need to be successful.

We'll discuss these topics more fully in Chapter 4: Culture of Communications.

Hold Everyone Accountable

Great performers like accountability; poor performers shrink from it. We will discuss this in detail in Chapter 8 on the Follow-up/Follow-through process. If you want to disrespect your great performers, don't distinguish between high and low performance. Failure to create accountability sends a clear message that performance doesn't matter and behavior outside your value set doesn't matter either. The old adage rings true, "You get what you demonstrate and what you tolerate." If you're going to tolerate less than adequate performance, that's what you'll get. And if, as a leader, you're demonstrating disrespectful behavior of any sort, or protecting others who do (even by looking away and ignoring it), there should be a special corner of leadership hell for you.

Bring Energy, Passion, and Optimism to Work Every Day

If leaders aren't energized and engaged, it's hard for anyone else to be energized and engaged. As an electric utility lineman once told us, "I don't know if enthusiasm is contagious, but I know that a lack of enthusiasm is definitely contagious."

Now that doesn't mean some sort of false enthusiasm where people don't talk about, or don't recognize, all the stuff that's not going well. The best environments embrace the paradox of celebrated discontent. They recognize reality. Nothing is ever perfect. The challenge to keep improving is never-ending. Their optimism stems from the undying belief that the organization and the people in it are resilient and can find solutions to whatever challenges they encounter.

ASSESS YOUR TALENT AND BENCH STRENGTH

The next part of Right, Right, Right is the responsibility to constantly assess and grow the capabilities of the people you have. If you want people to fully commit, they need to know that you will dedicate yourself to growing their capabilities as expectations change.

As we discussed earlier, we're all competing in a world of perpetual whitewater. The turbulence drives rapid changes in strategy, technology, and tactics to stay ahead of competitors. That means that leaders must commit to continually assessing, growing, and developing the capabilities of their people.

People want to be in environments that help them grow their skills. They leave places that don't help them grow. "Lack of growth potential" is a top reason people become dissatisfied with their jobs.

Assessing the Talent You Have: Performance and Potential

The first part of this is to realistically assess the talent you have. The best organizations have some sort of on-going talent review process. General Electric's Session C – which is their annual process for reviewing the talent throughout the organization – is maybe the most famous of these. Many other organizations have similar processes. Regardless of what your organization's process is, leaders at all levels need to constantly assess where their employees are today versus where they need to be both today and in the future for the organization to be successful.

Unfortunately, when we ask people to describe how they know someone on their team is ready for promotion, the most common answer is, "He's a good guy." Or, if we ask what it would take for someone to be ready to move to the next level, the most common answer is, "More time in their current role," without any commentary about what capabilities the person needs to develop or grow.

If you want to ensure a steady flow of qualified candidates into roles that help drive execution in your organization, you need a better structure for thinking through the performance in the current role, the potential for future roles and the capabilities that need to be developed or grown for both current and future roles. Then, that assessment needs to be connected to do a development plan for each member of your team.

Figure 2.1 shows a pretty typical 9-box grid for assessing the talent on your team on two critical dimensions: Performance in the current role and Potential for future job roles.

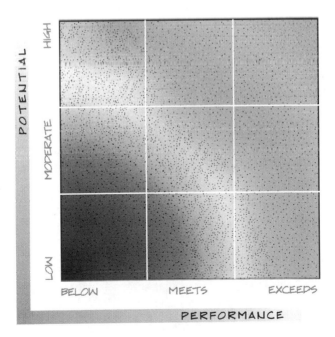

FIGURE 2.1
Assessing performance and potential: The 9-box grid.

There are a few critical issues to make this process work:

First, be clear with each of your team members about what great performance looks like in their current role. Obviously, much of this assessment will reflect performance versus their critical Result-Oriented Goals (which we discuss in Chapter 5), but it should also consider how well each team member supports and helps grow your organization's culture. As we discussed above, team members who deliver results but don't work well with others can create an enormous amount of disruption.

Next, assessing potential[1] requires an understanding of:

- The requirements of any future job role you foresee a team member moving to over time. Your regular assessments of each team member should include whether they're close to meeting the requirements for their *next* job.
- How the requirements of potential jobs are likely to change over time. What capabilities will the organization require one, three, or five years in the future? That then informs how you develop and grow people to meet those future requirements.

Potential is a moving target. As we've noted, the requirements of most jobs are changing and will continue to change on a rapid basis. So, part of the assessment, even within a current job role, needs to anticipate how that job will evolve over time. This, in turn, informs the development of the teammate in that role.

Make frank assessments of people and where they fit on the grid. Over the years, we've seen any number of leaders use the 2,2-box as some sort of purgatory for people on their teams. They'll say something like:

Performance meets expectations.
Potential is okay but not great (which means that the person is staying in this role for the foreseeable future, if not forever).

And that's okay if that's where they are. These are solid performers who might also be helping other people succeed.

---

[1] "Potential" in this sense means "opportunity to be promoted." But, people can demonstrate potential even within a given role. There are a ton of people who like the role they are in, but still kick butt in their role while they constantly adapt and adjust to changing job requirements.

What's not okay is using this as a default zone that enables the leader to avoid taking real action to either develop the person to their full potential or deal with an underperformer.

In one organization we worked with, management had a category labeled, "too soon to tell," which made sense for people who had just moved into a new role. However, it was pretty odd when we started to see the same people in the "too soon to tell" category one, two, or even three years later. Clearly, their leaders had stuck those people into the "too soon to tell" category because they didn't want to address some issue or another.

Effective talent assessment should be seen as the platform for growth. But even though everyone knows the Ken Blanchard/Rick Tate quote, "Feedback is the Breakfast of Champions," when we ask, "How do you know how well you're performing in your job?" the number one answer is, "I must be doing okay. I'm not getting in any trouble."

The outcome of your assessment must inform the conversations you have with your team members about both their performance and their potential. Often, we see a huge disconnect between the talent assessment conversation and what gets fed back to the team member. We'll discuss this in the section on Courageous Conversations in Chapter 4.

To be clear, we are not advocating that leaders share with their team members their actual potential rating during development conversations with each team member. We ARE advocating that leaders be very clear about what the team member needs to do to continue to grow his/her capabilities to be ready to move to some future job. So, that would look far more like "This Conversation" as outlined below, and "Not That Conversation" (Table 2.1).

Those are very different conversations. "This Conversation" gives the team member the guidance he/she needs to develop their capabilities and prepare for the future role. And, while the leader can support the team member, the ball is left in the team member's court to take advantage of development opportunities. The "Not That Conversation" merely reassures the team member that a future promotion is a matter of time in the role. Not only does that not give the team member what they need to grow, it also sets up future disappointment if others get promoted before this team member after he/she thinks they have had enough time in the role.

TABLE 2.1

Feedback for Growing Talent...

This Conversation...	...Not That Conversation
So, you're interested in becoming a Supervisor. Here are the things you need to work on: 1. Often, when you have disagreements with others, you can become overly assertive (Cite examples). While having your point of view is good, there are times that you need to resolve conflict in a more collaborative manner. Here are a couple opportunities to develop those skills. 2. You have performed very well and hit your goals very consistently. However, what I don't see is you taking a leadership role with the rest of your team. Let's discuss what you can do to informally lead when it's appropriate and get you engaged in a couple opportunities to lead a project to help you build some of those capabilities.	Yeah, I know you'd like to get promoted to Supervisor. You're doing okay. You just need more time in this role. You'll be great.

Getting the Wrong People Off the Bus

As critical as it is to have the right people in the right roles with the right capabilities, it's also necessary to get the wrong people off the bus or to move them into roles where they can perform well. The "9-box framework" can provide guidance about who those people might be and how you might deal with them.

People who fall into the low performance range at the left-hand side of the grid require these questions:

Is this person in the right role on the bus?
Should this person be on the bus?

In the low-performance, low-potential block of the grid, leaders need to make an active decision about whether someone ought to even be in the organization. If you decide they can stay in the short run, you must either have a plan in place to get performance to an acceptable level or manage them out of the organization by whatever process your organization has.

In the other two boxes in the left-hand side, you may have more latitude in terms of options, but you still have to actively manage the situation. In these two boxes, you have people who are underperforming in their current role but still have some potential for future roles. It's a legitimate question to ask whether they are in the wrong role, or if there is some issue in the current role that is preventing them from being as successful as they ought to be. (A good place to start that thinking is with the Performance Gears outlined in Chapters 5 through 8 in this book!)

Of course, if you have someone underperforming, but you believe they have the potential for future roles, you have to think carefully through how you'll manage that situation. You certainly don't want to set a precedent of rewarding underperformers for their lack of performance, but you also want to provide your team the greatest opportunity to be successful and make a meaningful contribution.

BUILD CAPABILITIES: DEVELOPMENT THAT WORKS

Finally, you have to develop people to perform better in the roles they are in both for today and in the future. Let's start with the honest truth that many organizations mess up the development piece badly.

First, we often don't devote enough time or energy to developing the team. Think about how much time sports teams, bands, orchestras, or dance troupes spend practicing versus how much time they spend actually in front of audiences. In endeavors that require great performance, the performers spend more time on the practice field than they do on the playing field.

In most work settings, it's exactly the opposite. We spend almost all of our time on the playing field and very little time on the practice field. While it's impractical and unrealistic to think that you should spend more time practicing than playing, it is realistic to think that performers in our organizations should spend more than 1% or 2% of their time improving their capabilities to perform.

That does not mean, however, that people in your organization can't make tremendous strides through practice. In Chapter 7 on Performance Drivers, we will discuss "Deliberate Practice." We'll wait until then to get into the details, but the idea is that the right coach can distill best practices in almost any field, skills and approaches that might have taken the field's highest achievers years or even decades to develop, and make those best practices accessible to the rest of us.

Second, we compound the challenge because what we do on the practice field often seems disconnected from what we do on the playing field. People are sent to training for the sake of training, not because there is necessarily some specific capability they are supposed to develop or grow. Can you imagine a highly successful sports coach like Alabama's Nick Saban NOT having a specific learning objective for every player for every minute of every practice?

I can't tell you how many times we've had conversations like the following when facilitating training sessions:

Facilitator: Why are you here?
Participant: I got the email.
Facilitator: Huh?
Participant: Yeah, I'm here because I got this email that I was supposed to be in XYZ class today.
Facilitator: OK. Let me try a different question. What do you want to learn in this program?
Participant: Don't know. What's this class about? It sounds interesting. But, I'm only here because I got the email ... this morning.

In spite of this rough start, we're constantly amazed at how much people want to learn, even when they are thrust into situations only because they "got the email."

We call that Learning by Coincidence. They're in a training session. We happen to say something that intrigues them. The words seem to fly past their ears, they are intrigued by the thoughts and they capture them.

There has to be a better way.

There is. Humans are natural learners. They want to get better at whatever intrigues them. Witness:

- A 1-year old learning to walk. He/she is a bundle of unstoppable energy. Pulling himself/herself up on the sofa or coffee table or whatever in reach will cause the most damage! Falling down. Then getting right back up and doing it all over again until he/she really can walk.

- The 2-year old learning cause and effect by dropping a toy at the dinner table and then waiting for someone to pick the toy up and hand it back. So, the toddler drops it again. Waits for the other person to pick it up. Which the toddler then drops again … all the time learning, "Hey, if I do this, I can get that reaction".
- Millions, if not billions, of people every day who turn to YouTube to learn how to make a recipe, fix a car, or unplug a toilet.

These are all incredibly effective learning models.

So, how do we embed the same kind of learning into developing the full capabilities of people in our organizations? We call it the ABC model as shown in Figure 2.2:

FIGURE 2.2
The ABC model of effective learning processes.

A – is what goes on before any learning experience.
B – is the learning experience.
C – is what happens after the experience.

What we've learned is that if A and C are managed well, then B will be successful. The learners will learn, even demand to learn, what they need from the session.

If A and C aren't managed effectively, no matter how great the actual learning experience (B), the amount of transfer back to work is purely coincidental.

To make the A part of the process work as effectively as possible, consider the following issues.

Set the Foundation

The learner and his manager need to engage in effective conversations about the learner's growth and development needs, preferably as part of an on-going conversation.

Set the Expectations

The learner and her manager should discuss expectations for what the learner needs to take away from any learning event before the event. What are the one or two most critical outcomes from this session?

This expectation-setting process often should also include the session facilitator, coach, etc. Those expectations should tie as directly back to the learner's growth and development plan as possible.

Active Preparation

We also advocate active preparation before any learning event, even if that preparation is merely to write down the learner's expectations for the event. Writing down the expectations is essentially making a contract about what the takeaways should be.

In short:

- How is the learner engaged in setting expectations for the learning experience?
- What expectations does the learner set before he/she goes to the class?
- How does his/her manager communicate what the session is going to be about and how that fits with his/her overall development plan?
- What active preparation does the learner engage in prior to the session to be most ready to capture the benefits and apply them to his/her efforts?

B – is what happens during the learning event itself.

This would include what the learner's participation looks like in a training session (virtual or classroom), a coaching session or any other learning event. C – is what happens after the session.

In most learning situations, the answer to that question is: "Nothing." People go back to work and do exactly what they were doing before the learning experience. Heck, they're usually behind on their "real work" from having been engaged in the session, so they jump back into the fray and immediately forget what the session was about.

In worst-case scenarios, and we've seen more than a few, the participant's manager or others actively undermine the learning event with comments like, "Forget all the crap you heard in that training session. That's not how we do it out here in the real world."

The critical issue is to reinforce the learning and to integrate it into on-going work as quickly as possible.

To make the learning as effective and as transferable as possible, it's best when the learner and his/her manager de-brief the event with a variation of the 5-Minute/5-Question conversation that we cover more fully in the Follow-up/Follow-through chapter.

- What were the goals/expectations for the learning event?
- What were the top 3–5 things you took away from the event related to those expectations?
- What did you learn that would re-shape your thinking in any way?
- What will you do differently to improve performance (or to prepare for some future opportunity)?
- How can we measure how effectively you applied the learning?
- When will we follow up again regarding your takeaways from the session and how you've applied them to your work?

If learners understand going into any kind of learning session that there will be consistent follow-up and reinforcement, the probability of the learners applying what they've learned goes up dramatically, which then increases the probability that performance will improve as a result of the learning effort. It also subtly reinforces the concept that the organization is committed to developing people in the organization to be their best. It's not training for the sake of training, it's training for the sake of both the learner and the organization.

You might have noticed that we gave B short shrift. Here's why: When A and C are actively managed, what happens in B almost doesn't matter! The quality of the session facilitator or coach hardly matters. The learner – knowing the expectations and knowing she is accountable for the learning – will stick with it, keep asking questions, etc., until she gets what she needs.

Now, the coach or facilitator may never get asked back – ineptitude doesn't lead to repeat work! – but the learner will get what he needs.

On the other hand, when A (Before) and C (After) are ignored, all of the emphasis goes to B (The Learning Experience). Any learning is coincidental. The facilitator or coach says something. The learner is intrigued by it, maybe writes down the thought and then, really maybe, does something with the thought when he/she goes back to the real work. For the coach or session facilitator, they often – at least temporarily – devolve down to "Enter-trainment" (sing a song, dance a lick, try to be funny, see if you can keep the participants entertained for the duration of the session because they clearly are not there with any expectations about what they want or need to learn).

Developing People to Handle Tomorrow's Whitewater

It's a dynamic world. Job requirements change quickly. Many of the jobs our kids will perform don't exist today. The jobs that most people perform today will either change dramatically or disappear completely over the course of their careers.

We met a person driving a cab recently who served as a great example of the constantly evolving nature of work. When we met him, he was driving a cab in Fort Lauderdale. When asked why he was driving a cab, he said, "Well, my previous job was essentially eliminated by technology. I used to be a graphic artist and I was responsible for the work that went into preparing magazine covers. But that work we did by hand was replaced by people using Adobe Photoshop and similar programs. Then I moved to Florida and became a cabby. But this work is going to be replaced by technology, too. Uber and Lyft are driving cabs out of the market. So, I'm going to be displaced out of this, too."

He's not atypical. It's pretty much a guarantee that whatever skills and capabilities people on your team have, they will be outmoded within a few years. If you want to execute effectively and keep up with rapidly changing job requirements, you have to commit to helping the people on your team adapt their capabilities as requirements change. This places a special burden on leaders to:

- Understand what's required.
- Understand where their team members are.
- Help them get what they need to grow/change their capabilities.
- Be patient enough to let them develop while creating accountability for the growth.

THOUGHT STARTER QUESTIONS

1. How well do people feel they are fully engaged in the organization and its purpose?
2. To what extent do they feel the organization makes the best possible use of their talents?
3. How clear is what you're looking for in new team members from both a technical/functional skill set and for fit to the values-set?
4. How much emphasis do you place on technical/functional skills versus values-fit in your recruitment and selection efforts?
5. To what extent do they feel the company invests in them to aid their transitions to new responsibilities/requirements?
6. What feedback are people getting to help them be their best?
7. How far in the future are you looking to see what skills and capabilities will be required for future success? What skills and abilities will become outmoded? How are you helping your team to prepare for this change?
8. How effective are your development efforts? How well do you manage the ABC process for effective development?

FIRST STEPS

1. Define your Playing Field.

   What's the mission/purpose of your group? What values do you want people to play by to support that mission? If your organization has a well-established set of values, are there any additional "Key Characteristics" that members of your team need to exhibit to best enable your success?

2. Assess your organization's environment.

   How engaging is it?

3. Assess your team.

   Use the 9-box grid and rate the performance and potential of each member of your team.

Based on where they are, what are the capabilities each team member most needs to grow?

4. Commit to a better approach to team member growth and development.

Make sure everyone is getting the feedback they need to be their best.

Utilize the A→B→C process for more effective development.

Set learning objectives with each team member before they engage in any learning experience.

Reinforce the learning experience with de-briefs and regular Follow-up/Follow-through.

BIBLIOGRAPHY

Blanchard, Kenneth & Johnson, Spencer (1982). *The One Minute Manager*. New York, NY: William Morrow and Company, Inc.

Blanchard, Kenneth, Zigarmi, Patricia & Zigarmi, Drea (1985). *Leadership and the One Minute Manager*. New York, NY: William Morrow and Company, Inc.

Brinkerhoff, Robert O. & Apking, Anne M. (2001). *High Impact Learning*. Cambridge MA: Perseus.

Einstein, Albert. (1956). *Out of My Later Years: The Scientist, Philosopher and Man Portrayed Through his Own Words*. New York, NY: Citadel Press.

Ericsson, Anders & Pool, Robert. (2016). *Peak: Secrets from the New Science of Expertise*. New York, NY: Houghton Mifflin Harcourt.

Iverson, Ken. (1998). *Plain Talk*. New York, NY: John Wiley & Sons, Inc.

Marshall, Penny (Director). (1992). *A League of Their Own*. Sony Pictures.

Patterson, Kerry, Grenny, Joseph, McMillan, Ron & Switzler, Al. (2002). *Crucial Conversations*. New York, NY: McGraw-Hill.

Peters, Thomas J. & Waterman, Jr., Robert H. (1982). *In Search of Excellence*. New York, NY: Harper & Row.

Quinn, Robert E. (1996). *Deep Change: Discovering the Leader Within*. San Francisco, CA: Jossey-Bass.

3

Align the Architecture: Creating Organizational Gravity

Why does it feel like it flows like the tides some days and other days it's just a total struggle?

Ron Dickerson, former VP and GM at Nucor

A TALE OF TWO PRODUCTION LINES

Bad Architecture...

A manufacturing facility we worked with had identified and engineered a change to a production line that would cut costs and improve productivity. The organization was marginally profitable, so this was an important win for them.

The production line change was relatively simple and could be accomplished over a weekend. Yet the project was delayed multiple times over the next several months. Many people inside the organization were confused why a simple change was taking months to complete. When the company looked deeper to find the cause, they discovered that the production supervisor had been delaying it. He was dragging his heels because the change was going to decrease his bonus compensation. Even though the company was much better off, doing the right thing for the organization was actually punishing the supervisor.

...Great Architecture

Contrast that with a Nucor steel mill we visited a few years ago. The mill was in the middle of a major shutdown, yet the supervisors and managers I spent time with seemed to have nothing more important to do than chat with me. I've been in more than a few manufacturing facilities during shutdowns, and generally, the scene is pandemonium. Everyone is scrambling to get the plant up and running. When I remarked upon this, one of the department managers I was with said, "Look, the team knows what to do. They've been involved in the preparation. They know the job is to complete the necessary tasks as safely and as quickly as possible. And their production bonuses incent them to do the right things to get the mill running quickly and safely. As leaders, we don't need to be running around like crazy people micro-managing the process."

In the first plant, the organization's architecture pushed against the supervisor doing the right thing for the organization, so the change was slow and cumbersome. In the Nucor mill, the change happened quickly, in part because the organization's architecture was well aligned with the desired outcomes.

Time and again, we find that when we align an organization's architecture – the systems, structures, processes, and culture – to its strategy, execution of the strategy "flows like the tides."

An organization's systems, structures, processes, and culture create what we call organizational gravity. They provide an enormous, relentless, and yet often-unseen influence over the decisions and actions every team member makes every minute. When those forces are aligned to the strategy, then execution of the strategy flows. When they are misaligned, execution of the strategy fights against those forces. The misalignment creates friction that slows, or in the worst cases completely disrupts, execution of the strategy.

It's impossible for an organization to orchestrate the actions of each individual, as the situation on the ground changes monthly, weekly, or even hourly. Impossible and not even desirable. The organization's frontline leaders and performers need to have the latitude and responsibility to make rapid decisions in response to quickly changing competitive and operational factors. As competitive strategy evolves at an ever-faster pace in response to fast-changing business environments, organizations often find their systems, structures, processes, and culture aligned to an out-of-date strategy. Frontline execution falls out of touch with what the business requires for success.

When the architecture is misaligned with the strategy and objectives of the organization, the forces of gravity pull against the strategic intent. As a result, execution of the strategy is inconsistent, slow, and unresponsive to rapid changes in the competitive environment. People may default to old habits. Like the production line supervisor above, they pursue what they are rewarded for, even if those actions are misaligned with the strategy.

Sometimes the architecture encourages inaction, rather than counter-productive action. It can be as simple and as subtle as this: back in high school, a friend of mine named Tim worked on a construction crew for the summer. He was young, athletic, and energetic. The first couple of days on the job he was busting his tail and outworking the more experienced, full-time members of the crew. Near the end of the second day, one of the grizzled veterans pulled him aside and said in no uncertain terms, "Son, you need to slow your ass down." When Tim inquired why, the vet was clear: "Because you're making the rest of us look bad." The architecture of the organization, in this case the underlying culture, highly influenced Tim to slow down, which clearly was not in the best interest of the construction firm.

On the flip side, what was the veteran's reward system? He was paid hourly. So, the more hours he worked, the more he got paid. The pay structure encouraged him to drag work out as long as he could without getting himself fired. His reward system was completely not aligned with the interest of the construction company.

Over the years, we've seen dozens of examples where the organizational architecture was misaligned with the strategic intent of the organization, resulting in slow, inconsistent execution:

- A general manager in an organization we worked with was asked to integrate more effectively with a sister division. He understood it was the right thing to do. And his bonus incentives rewarded him for doing it. He told us, "But, my boss has told me that keeping my job is based on how *my* division performs." As a result, the integration took years instead of months. In the meantime, the company ceded market share to its competitors and suffered eroding profit margins.
- Sales and service reps in another company we worked with were paid based 100% on their individual performance. The strategy of the company, once focused on simply acquiring as many customers as possible, evolved into delivering superior service to its customers.

This change required those reps to coordinate with each other. But their compensation unequivocally rewarded individual accomplishment. Until the compensation changed, their behavior didn't change. Once the compensation system was more fully aligned with the evolved strategy of the organization, the sales and service reps changed their behavior within weeks.

In each of these cases, the companies suffered from organizational friction caused by organizational architecture aligned in the wrong direction. In each case, they tried to live with it rather than fix it, until the friction became almost unbearable. That's understandable. Changing the architecture IS the hard stuff ... which we'll discuss in more depth at the end of this chapter.

Since this is the hard stuff, we've built this chapter around a few of the classic W and H questions, with one bonus question at the end:

WHO? Leader as Organizational Architect
WHAT? Aligning Systems, Structures, Processes, and Culture to Create
    Organization Gravity
WHEN? Knowing When to Change the Architecture
HOW? Design Principles for Aspiring Architects

Plus…

WHAT ELSE? This is the Hard Stuff.

WHO? LEADER AS ORGANIZATIONAL ARCHITECT

We were working with a leader taking his organization through a significant transformation. Every day the executive could see, hear, and feel dozens of challenges his organization faced. He was exhausted from playing organizational whack-a-mole, trying to squash each challenge as it popped up. He felt like he was the only person playing the game. Others in the organization were creating the challenges, not trying to squash them.

We've seen dozens of leaders in a wide variety of organizations facing similar challenges. Like the executive we just mentioned, they can solve any one, five, or even ten of the problems their organizations face. But they can't solve them all. For that, they need to get the rest of the organization playing whack-a-mole alongside them.

It's the responsibility of leaders to create organizational gravity. But leaders often don't see themselves as architects of their organization's systems, structures, processes, and culture. They've often inherited architecture that has worked – sometimes phenomenally well – for years. So, when the strategy shifts, they don't necessarily see the need to change the architecture. Like Albert Einstein wrote,[1] "What does a fish know about the water in which he swims all his life?" It's hard to manage a force you don't recognize. So, when the architecture falls out of alignment, leaders often see only the symptoms, not the underlying cause of problems.

Because they focus on the symptoms, leaders will sometimes default to making goal-oriented proclamations like, "We need to deliver better service to customers." Or "Grow sales in this market" or "cut costs" without understanding the headwinds created by an architecture that is misaligned with those statements. Or they will say, "People just need to take ownership" or "Everyone needs to work together." While both might be true statements, merely saying them doesn't change organizational gravity. So, behavior is unlikely to change. If the systems, structures, or processes reward independent contribution instead of working together, the people who do try to take ownership will only end up frustrated.

So, you're a leader and you think your architecture might need some realignment. The next question is...

WHAT? ALIGNING SYSTEMS, STRUCTURES, PROCESSES, AND CULTURE TO CREATE ORGANIZATIONAL GRAVITY

There are four primary elements of architecture that must be aligned to create organizational gravity that pulls the organization in the direction of your strategy: Systems, Structures, Processes, and Culture.

We'll briefly discuss each of them.

---

[1] 1995, Out of My Later Years, Albert Einstein, Chapter 2: Self-Portrait (Essay dated 1936), Citadel Press Book: Carol Publishing Group, New York.

Systems

Organizational systems support the growth and maintenance functions of the organization. Systems like talent acquisition, growth and development, and promotion dramatically influence the values, culture, and capabilities of the organization. Systems like information technology strongly influence who has what information, which in turn helps determine where and when decisions are made. Performance measurement, compensation, recognition, and reward systems send powerful messages about what's important to the organization.

WANT TEAMWORK? CHANGE YOUR TALENT MANAGEMENT AND SUCCESSION PLANNING SYSTEMS

Another organization we worked with wanted to make a significant shift away from purely individual contribution to a more team-oriented approach. They found themselves struggling to make the shift. Ultimately though, they changed their compensation system to reflect the new strategic priorities. They also changed their recruitment and selection processes to find people who were more team-oriented (without sacrificing the critical technical/functional capabilities they needed to be successful). Finally, they also aligned their talent management and succession planning systems to promote leaders more aligned with the company's strategy. As those systems and processes came into alignment, the "unseen" forces began to pull the organization in the direction they wanted to go.

Ask Yourself

In thinking about your major organizational systems like compensation, rewards and recognition, talent management, and promotions, it might be helpful to ask yourself some of these questions:

How aligned are they to your strategy and strategic goals? Do the right people get rewarded for doing the right things?

How well does your compensation system in all parts of the organization reward people for delivering results consistent with the strategy?

How strong is your bench? Do you have enough of the right people to support your strategy – people who both share the organization's core values AND have the capabilities to execute effectively?

To what extent do your organization's growth and development efforts help people build the capabilities you will need for success in the future?

Who gets promoted? Are people promoted for delivering short-term results at the expense of others and/or your long-term strategic objectives?

Structures

The formal structure defines the hierarchical arrangement of the organization. It's represented by the organizational chart: Who reports to whom and how the organization is organized – by function, by geography, etc. The formal structure lays out roles and responsibilities and defines, to a great extent, how work is assigned and coordinated. It resolves issues like:

- Whether you're a typical hierarchical organization or more of a matrixed organization.
- How work is accomplished, emphasizing independent contribution or teamwork.
- How people are connected to each other across organizational boundaries.
- How much latitude and responsibility are delegated to team members?
- Whether organizational control is centralized or decentralized.

In general, organizational structure needs to allow for ever-faster and more flexible decision-making to keep pace with the quickly evolving speed of the competitive environment.

Ask Yourself

How well does your structure focus responsibility and accountability on specific individuals or teams?

To what extent do the responsible individuals and teams have the latitude they need to act?

How often do you see things fall between the cracks of your organization? How often do people point fingers at each other for not delivering results or hitting goals or other commitments? How often do people say, "That's not my job" or "Not our responsibility?"

How often do you see different parts of the organization in conflict with each other due to turf wars?

Q: What's It Take to Get a Cup of Coffee?
A: Blow Up the Organization!

We worked with a resort that had a vast array of properties, including a restaurant attached to its golf shop. The restaurant opened at 8 a.m. Early bird golfers would arrive at 6:30 a.m. and find they couldn't get a cup of coffee before starting their round. Why? Because the resort was organized by function. The food and beverage people were responsible for the coffee in the restaurant, and they had no interest in opening the restaurant before 8 a.m. That would just stretch their personnel, drive up their costs, and make their internal reports look worse.

The resort suffered multiple problems because of this structure. In another example, the golf shop's carpets were dirty many mornings, because another functional group, housekeeping, kept a schedule that brought them to the shop in the afternoon.

The team members in the golf shop realized the negative impact this was having on their customers, who grumbled that they couldn't get a simple cup of coffee for an early tea time or were put off by a messy golf shop if they happened to stop by in the morning. But no one felt they could fix the problems – until they realigned the structure.

They blew up the organization. Jobs were no longer organized by function. Instead, they created dozens of small business units throughout the resort, including a golf shop "business unit." Once the workers in the golf shop became responsible for the shop's performance as a mini-business, they made sure golfers could get coffee at early hours and carpets were clean throughout the day.

The transformation was quick and thorough. Team members took "ownership" of their "businesses" and improved performance for both guests and the organization.

Processes

Processes define the steps your organization takes to complete its work. This includes external facing processes like order to cash for customer transactions or your procurement process from ordering from suppliers to paying them. Who does what in what sequence to take a customer's order, process it, ship it, and bill for it? Internally, how does the organization identify the need for raw materials, order them, receive them, warehouse them, and make them ready for delivery? How does the organization procure, maintain, and dispose of its property, plant(s), and equipment?

"Walk through" your organization's most critical processes, especially those that touch the customer. Then...

Ask Yourself

How easy is it for customers to buy from you?

How easy is it for them to check on order status?

Where are the bottlenecks, if any, in your fulfillment process?

How easy is it to return a product or get a refund for a service that didn't meet expectations?

How easy is it for customers to make a complaint?

What happens to the complaints that customers do make?

Do you have a process to identify significant recurring problems and eliminate them?

Culture

Your culture describes what it's like to work for your organization. It's represented by the stories people tell of their experiences in the organization. It includes items like:

- How open and inclusive the organization is.
- What the work ethic is like.
- How much latitude people have to make decisions and act.
- What gets celebrated.
- What do people get in trouble for.
- How accountable do people feel.
- How centralized versus decentralized decision-making is.
- How much work is completed through team collaboration versus independent contribution.

- How energized people are by the organization and working with each other.
- The extent to which people feel they can contribute their best, etc.

If Values (as we talked about in the Right, Right, Right chapter) represent how the organization *should* align to the strategy, the Culture represents how the organization *does* align to the strategy.

A critical distinction: Aligning the culture to the strategy is not code for meaning that "everyone should look, think, and speak the same." It does mean having a value set that aligns to the execution of the organization's strategy and drives it forward. Thinking back to the Right, Right, Right chapter, it means having a culture that embodies Integrity, Trust, and Respect along with other values critical to the individual organization. The leader's role is to understand any gaps – and there is always some gap – between the espoused values and the actual culture of the organization. It's the role of leaders to identify those gaps, understand the causation, and actively work to close those gaps.

Ask Yourself

What stories do people tell about what it's like to work in your organization? How do those stories compare with what you hope they will say?

Do you have an engagement survey process in place? What are the key opportunities that have been identified?

What do online websites like Glassdoor.com say about what it's like to work in your organization? What processes do you have in place to understand this feedback at a deeper level and react to it as appropriate?

WHEN? KNOWING WHEN TO CHANGE THE ARCHITECTURE

If we wanted to be dramatic, we could have called this section "The Canary in the Coal Mine" or "When Your Spidey Senses Cause the Hair on the Back of Your Neck to Stand Up."

How do you know if your organizational architecture is preventing full, effective execution of your strategy?

Start with the premise that you should always be proactively assessing whether your current organizational architecture best supports your strategy and overall organizational goals. The odds of it being perfectly aligned to your strategy are pretty slim.

Here are a few questions that might indicate misalignment in the architecture:

- Can people at every level of the organization succinctly describe your strategy and outline the two or three most critical things they must do to help you succeed?
- Is it taking longer than you feel it should to execute your strategy?
- In spite of your best intentions, does execution fall short of your expectations?
    - Are you falling short on one or more dimensions of customer choice that are critical to your competitive advantage?
    - Do your customers say that your competitors are as good as or better than you at something you feel is critical to your competitive advantage?
- In spite of what you believe are crisp, clear communications (see Chapter 4: Creating a Culture of Communications) about your organization's strategy, do you see people taking actions that are aligned to an older strategy or clearly not aligned to your organization's success?
    - Are these isolated incidents or do you see a repeating pattern in multiple parts of your organization? We once worked with a group of regional sales managers in an organization. Those sales managers were supposed to work with each other to ensure they didn't inadvertently compete with each other in the pursuit of growing market share and profits with their customers. They would meet a few times a year to coordinate activities. They would always agree to cooperate. But as soon as they returned to their home markets, their regional vice presidents would remind them that they needed to take care of their region first …so they would go right back to competing with each other.
- Do any of your systems, structures, or processes reward the wrong behavior (like the production supervisor we discussed at the beginning of this chapter)?
- Do any of them punish people for acting consistently with the strategy?

TRUST FALLS ≠ TEAMWORK

We've seen dozens of organizations invest thousands of dollars in "team-building" events designed to get people to work together more effectively. They spend time on trust falls, walking on logs, or building tinker-toy towers. Almost invariably, everyone works together during the team-building event because really, no matter how much everyone despises Roy in Accounting, it is completely socially and morally unacceptable to let him fall during the trust fall. But, when they all get back to work the next day, they may be more than happy to let him "fall down on the job."

Why? Because what we don't usually talk about during team-building sessions is what are the things that cause people to not work together back at work, which in a lot of cases is the underlying systems, structures, processes, or culture that pull people away from working together.

So, do the team-building event if you want … they do often help people connect with each other better. But if you want better teamwork, fix the architecture too!

This can be very subtle. Several years ago, we were working with a grocery store chain that had positioned itself as providing superior service to its customers. In their marketing assessment work, it was clear that this was something customers valued and that the company could distinguish itself through delivering a better customer experience.

The leaders had learned in their research that customers valued it when they could ask team members questions about where to find items in the store and the team members would actually help them.

Part of our engagement included mystery shopping the client's stores to see how consistently they executed on various aspects of the customer experience. One of the things we studied was how store team members reacted to customers who seemed to need help finding items in the store.

The good news: Whenever we connected with team members, they were super-helpful in getting us to the right place in the store to find the items we were looking for.

The bad news: Most of the time when we entered aisles looking like we were trying to find something, team members literally scurried out the other end of the aisle. We were struck by how consistent the behavior was across stores, team members, and time of day.

Later, we conducted a focus group interview with the team members we had seen in the stores. When we asked them about this behavior, they were very open about why they ran away from us. They said, "Look, we know we're supposed to help customers find things in stores. And generally, we would be glad to do it. But here's the problem – every day when we start our shifts, our manager will give us a list of 10–20 things we have to accomplish that day." As if on cue, they all pulled that day's list from their pockets. "If we take the time to help 10 customers out each day, each one of them might take 5 minutes. That's 50 minutes or more out of our day. What that means is 2 or 3 items on our list don't get completed. At the end of the day, our managers don't ask us about the customers we helped and how that helped us deliver great service. They ask us why the hell we didn't get those 2 or 3 items completed."

HOW? DESIGN PRINCIPLES FOR ASPIRING (ORGANIZATIONAL) ARCHITECTS

The gravitational pull of the moon and sun are invisible forces that generate tides. How do we create organizational gravity – the often-unseen forces that pull performance toward the strategy? The more well aligned the systems, structures, processes, and culture are, the stronger the gravitational pull toward the purpose and strategy.

Recognizing that your organizational architecture may not be fully aligned with the strategic intent of your organization, how do you fix it? It would be impossible to be fully prescriptive of any changes in your organizational architecture in this book. (Or, frankly, in a dozen books.) There are thousands of books on organizational design, compensation design, etc.

However, it is possible to outline a set of design principles that apply to many, if not most, situations. They should provide a good starting point in your effort to align the unseen forces of organizational gravity to get execution to flow like the tides in your part of your organization:

1. The architecture needs to be actively aligned. It doesn't gravitate on its own.
2. Leaders need to change it enough to influence behavior that supports the desired culture and execution of the organization's strategy...
3. ...but not so much or so often that people are frustrated and confused.
4. Whenever possible, it's better to design changes WITH people, not TO them. The people affected by changes in architecture are often the ones who have the best ideas and perspective about what needs to change. Ultimately, they will be more committed to the change, and often the strongest evangelists, for having been involved in the design.
5. Engaging outsiders to provide expertise and to play devil's advocate is also often of value. For instance, we all think we are experts at compensation design. We're not. Restructuring organizations, compensation design, and other aspects of organizational architecture are as complex as performing surgery to remove an appendix. No one removes their own appendix, yet people will tinker with their compensation systems all day long, often creating disastrous consequences in the process.
6. Provide stability amid change. Changes to architecture can be disruptive and unsettling. People often have negative emotional reactions to change even when the changes will be positive. They wonder, "What's going to happen to me? Do I have what it takes to be successful in this new environment?" It's critical to provide a sense of stability. Consistent, focused, empathetic leadership goes a long way to helping people make transitions. As important, the organization's core values can provide an anchor that enables smoother transitions in architecture.
7. When designing the architecture, constantly strive to create ownership. Give responsibility and the latitude to act to the people closest in space and time to the work getting done, for example, actively selling or serving customers, frontline production team members. Doing so engages people and creates ownership for results while also boosting accountability.

8. The corollary to this: Eliminate control/accountability mismatches in which one person or group is accountable for results but an entirely different person or group controls the resources or decision-making authority to deliver those results.
9. Provide the most direct line of sight possible between effort and results (see Chapter 6: Build Visible Scorecards).
10. Eliminate all non-value-adding work. If people are tied up doing non-value-added work, changing the architecture merely moves the mess. It doesn't make it better just because it's someone else's responsibility now!
11. Be patiently impatient. There will be time delays between when you change the systems, structures, or processes. The trick is to not get so impatient that you layer changes on top of changes before the first set of changes has the chance to deliver improved results. The changes you make must ultimately deliver results. At the point that it's clear they won't, then it's time to consider other changes to the architecture.
12. Empathize and persevere. Some white blood cells inside the organization will fight any change. On the other hand, some changes do create legitimate unintended consequences that need to be surfaced and resolved. Recognize the difference between the two.
13. Be bold; grow a backbone! As we discuss in the next section, undertaking changes to the organizational architecture is not easy. They should not be undertaken lightly. But when they need to be changed, it's important. The changes need to be made with courage and conviction, not with a half-hearted, "I hope this works."

WHAT ELSE? THIS IS THE HARD STUFF

Redesigning the architecture feels like "the hard stuff." It feels risky. It often requires leaders to tear up things they may be most comfortable with, the "but we've always done it this way" stuff. As we said earlier, leaders often may not even recognize the systems, structures, processes, and cultural issues that are influencing the tides in the organization.

Fixing misalignment often requires a fundamental shake-up in how an organization goes about its business. That's difficult for any number of reasons:

- Sometimes leaders don't see the friction that's created by misalignment in the organizational architecture.
- Other times, we've seen leaders who implicitly accept the systems, structures, and processes that exist, not recognizing the role they could or should play in adapting them. It's a little like living next to the train tracks – visitors can't miss the sound of the train, but you rarely notice it.
- It can be frightening to start meddling with the systems, structures, processes, and, especially, culture of the organization. In many cases, leaders who need to make the changes have been successful specifically because of the systems, structures, processes, or culture they need to change. Or they may have close relationships with team members who will be jarred by the changes. As a leader, it's hard to feel confident about a change that by its nature is unfamiliar to everyone in the organization. The benefits will occur in the future while the discomfort of change is felt today.
- If changing the organizational architecture doesn't frighten people, it's rarely embraced right away, and often likely to piss them off.

People get used to their reporting structure. Changing that creates discomfort. As one general manager in the throes of a substantial reorganization told us, "I know it's the right thing to do. I just don't want to do it because of the impact it's going to have on me."

This goes double when the architecture change involves pay. People want to support their families. Changing compensation, even if it's to their benefit, generates fear of the unknown. We were working with a client through a compensation change for their sales team a few years ago. While the compensation change put a significant amount of their total compensation at risk, it was clear that any salesperson with a decent effort would greatly benefit (25% or more increases in total compensation). Those who excelled were likely to achieve 40%-plus increase. This had been clearly explained on multiple occasions.

Nonetheless, just before the new compensation system was about to go live, I happened to cross paths with two sales reps. They were completely freaked out by the new package. One talked about needing to change jobs because she was concerned about being able to pay her bills. Another talked about how his family was already cutting expenses in anticipation. As we discussed their concerns and they came to better understand the impact, their fears evaporated. But without that random encounter, their fear might have resulted in both making decisions that weren't in their, or their company's, best interest.

Sometimes, the people most threatened are the leaders in the middle of the organization. Effective execution generally requires delegating more responsibility and latitude to frontline team members. For leaders who are used to controlling the decision-making process, this can challenge their ability to lead and result in a significant resistance to change.

- The time delay between changes in architecture and recognizable results can create impatience and anxiety and erode commitment to the change.

Because aligning the architecture feels both harder and riskier, it's easy to ignore or dismiss the opportunity costs of not making the necessary changes. It's like chronic back pain … it's painful, but you can make it through the day. So, you put off doing anything more invasive to permanently fix the pain.

When the architecture is misaligned, you're likely to feel the pain, but you might disregard it. "It can't really be that bad. We can live with this." In the meantime, …

- Your organization is not executing your strategy.
- You're not fully capturing the competitive position you've staked out for your organization.
- You're not earning the returns you ought to from a fully executed strategy, which means…
- …you're also not accumulating the returns you need to invest in your organization for the future.
- People in the organization see the misalignment and question how committed you are to the strategy…
- …which subtly causes people to wonder if you're serious about anything you say is critical for the organization's success.

You may see the symptoms and feel the pain, but because of the fear of taking action, you choose to put up with it. You don't seek out the "treatment" that you need to execute at full speed. Some organizations can tolerate this kind of "chronic underperformance" for a while. For others, it's the beginning of a death spiral. They begin to hopscotch from one strategy or one solution that they don't fully implement to the next, hoping that things will get better.

As the book *Deep Change: Discovering the Leader Within*[2] by Robert E. Quinn demonstrates, people and organizations have an almost infinite capacity to ignore the chronic ache of a situation that needs change for fear of the sharp, but likely transient, pain of addressing the problem – especially because deep change, or changing the architecture, doesn't guarantee success. The choice isn't always obvious, but the consequences are critical: You can choose to tolerate the ache and carry on, even though the pain might gradually get worse. Or you can take on the sharp pain of realigning the architecture in hopes of executing your strategy to the fullest.

So, as one great leader we know told her team one day, "Suck it up, Buttercup." Sometimes you have to make the really difficult, seemingly risky decision to change the organizational architecture to get the results you want from your strategy!

THOUGHT STARTER QUESTIONS

1. What do people get recognized and rewarded for in your group or your organization? How well do those recognitions and rewards encourage people to deliver on the company's strategy and key strategic objectives?
2. How well is your compensation system aligned with your strategy and strategic objectives?
3. What gets people promoted? How well are the criteria for promotion aligned with your strategy, strategic objectives, and core values?
4. How well are your recruiting, selection, and hiring processes providing you with the talent you need to be successful and with people who share and execute the organization's core values?

---

[2] *Deep Change: Discovering the Leader Within*, Robert E. Quinn, Jossey-Bass, San Francisco, 1996.

5. How effectively is your talent management process:
   - Assessing your bench strength and identifying critical gaps?
   - Informing talent development efforts both for individuals and the organization to target growth in the most critical areas?
   - Identifying capabilities required for success in the future and then building them into your recruitment, selection, and development processes?
6. What stories do people tell of what it's like to work in your organization or your part of the organization? How well do those stories align with your strategy, your organization's values, and your view of what you hope they would say about it?
7. What stupid rules, policies, and procedures does your organization have that frustrate your customers, team members, or both? (And, yeah, everybody has some!)

FIRST STEPS

1. Talk to your customers.
   - What are the factors that cause them to choose you over your competitors?
   - How well do they perceive your execution of those choice factors versus their other best suppliers or your competitors or what they hope would happen?
   - How well aligned is the organization to deliver on those customer choice factors?
2. Conduct a mini-organizational assessment. Look for how well the organization's architecture is aligned to the strategic intent.
3. Walk through your customer-facing processes.
4. Conduct open, roundtable discussions with your team members. Find out:
   - How well compensation and other systems are aligned with executing your organization's strategy.
   - If they are ever rewarded for doing the wrong thing.
   - If they are ever punished for doing the right thing.
   - What processes most frustrate them in their efforts to deliver results for the organization and its customers?

4

Culture of Communications: Changing Marshmallows to Unicorns

The Marshmallow...

I first witnessed this early in my career, although since then I've seen it dozens of times in multiple organizations from as small as two or three levels to multi-national behemoths.

While at Pacific Gas and Electric, I often had a lot of mobility across the organization. One day I might meet with the CEO or one of the Executive Vice Presidents or Business Unit Leaders; the next day I'd be in my home division working with our frontline team members. I was often struck by how similar the conversations were:

> We have to improve the timeliness and quality of our service delivery to our customers.
> We have to drive out bureaucracy and give people the latitude to act.
> We have to get more efficient and drive down unnecessary costs.

Everyone saw the need for change, but, and it's a big BUT, the conversations were completely separate and distinct. The CEO, for example, knew we needed to deliver better customer experiences, but he didn't know the details behind why service delivery was so slow.

People at the frontline of the organization – customer service reps, technical salespeople, engineers, and construction team members – also knew service was too slow. It often took 20–25 weeks to connect new electric and gas service lines to customers, but developers could often put up a building much faster. The engineers were saying they used to be able to sketch out a plan and install a service in a few days or a couple of weeks. It was the computerized procedures, along with other bureaucratic processes which management installed, that added months to the setup process.

The CEO's message, in spite of his best efforts, didn't penetrate to the frontline team; the frontline team had almost no way to get their thinking and messages to the CEO. The consequences:

> The CEO was frustrated that the organization wasn't executing as well as it could or changing as fast as it needed to.
> The frontline team was frustrated that no one was listening or seeing the stupid stuff they had to deal with every day. And they felt that leaders didn't understand or care about the bureaucracy's negative impact on service delivery and efficiency.

These were the same conversations in a different language and completely disconnected from each other. The results were okay, but far short of what was possible. And everyone was frustrated.

We call this communications morass the Marshmallow Layer, the ooey gooey mass in the middle of most organizations that absorbs information and energy instead of transforming them into execution. Instead of getting passed along, the information gets stuck.

And here's the kicker: No one sets out to prevent information from moving. It just happens, in organizations of every size.

...and the Unicorn

We had an opportunity to visit an operation at FedEx Supply Chain a few years ago led by former Army Captain John Coleman. Coleman's unit had been recognized throughout the company for being a "high performing site." Company leaders wanted to better understand what made it so high performing.

We started our process by interviewing team members at the site. Virtually everyone told us the same thing:

Team member: This is a wonderful place to work. Best place I've ever worked.
Interviewer: What makes it that way?
Team member: It's the leadership. They make sure we understand what's going on. We can ask any questions we want, and people will

take the time to answer them and really explain to us what's happening and why. They listen to our ideas. We know if somebody comes up with a good idea to improve the process or take better care of our customers, they'll listen to us and just do it. And we get lots of feedback, much of it instantaneous, about how we're performing.

The stories people told us were so strikingly similar that we thought we had been set up. Nope, they were on the level. Everyone in the organization really did communicate that way all the time.

As one of the members of our interview team said, "We just crossed paths with the Unicorn," the mythical unseen creature of untold grace and beauty.

So, what does it take to transform a Marshmallow into a Unicorn?

Whatever "it" is, it eludes a lot of people. "The biggest challenge facing our organization is communication." Or, "It's a communication problem." Hell, yeah, because it's always a communication problem! Communication, or lack of, is one of the most critical issues facing most organizations. In many organizations, "communications" is one of the lowest rated items on employee engagement or culture surveys.

It's clear that leaders want to communicate well. They just don't know how to do it. And … maybe they're afraid. To truly communicate in a way that builds performance requires some guts. It requires identifying the problem, *confronting* the problem publicly without pulling punches, and continuing to call out the problem until it's solved. It is always easier to let it slide, so most leaders do. But then the problem lingers and festers until skirting it requires enormous effort. All the while, the organization suffers.

We've identified five elements critical to creating a "culture of communications" and dig deep to fully understand each one in the rest of this chapter. Each requires a little more fortitude than the previous one, as the communications get more and more personal. But they're all necessary for your organization to perform at its best.

They are:

1. Communicate, Communicate, Communicate: Once is Not Enough.
2. Setting the Foundation for a Culture of Communication: Integrity, Trust, and Respect.
3. Engaging in the Conversation.

4. "Feedback is the Breakfast of Champions" ... as long as you're willing to eat it.
5. Courageous Communications.

COMMUNICATE, COMMUNICATE, COMMUNICATE: ONCE IS NOT ENOUGH

I've fallen into this trap dozens of times. I bet you have, too.

> "I told them. I don't know why they aren't doing it."
> How many times did you tell them?
> "Once. They're adults. How many times should I have to tell them?"
> Clearly, more than once.

Why is that? We're all busy as can be. We're not hearing you because we're worried about the stuff we have to do when we get back to our desks; we have calls and emails to return; and, dang it, the babysitter just cancelled for tonight, so I have to sort that out. What did you say again?

We multi-task, even though experts tell us this is a bad idea.

We filter stuff out. We hear what we like and agree with. The rest just gets blocked.

We speak in different dialects. The people in receiving use different jargon from the folks in customer service. The baby boomers talk about Jimi Hendrix; the millennials Beyoncé. The Southerners and Northerners can't agree on what barbecue is.

Maybe we can't hear you over the traffic or machinery or the web conference audio connection static or other environmental factors.

And even if we hear you, we're probably not listening until you tell us the impact on us. While you are carefully articulating Why We're Doing This, each of us is having an internal monologue that goes something like, "What's going to happen to me? Do I still have a job? Can I be successful? What will I have to do differently? Who will I report to? Wait, what did you say again?"

Now that I've written these last few paragraphs, I think the title of this section ought to be:

Communicate
Communicate
Communicate
Communicate
Communicate
Communicate
Communicate
Communicate
Communicate

Consistency and repetition are key. Strive to overcommunicate:

- What we're doing
- Why we're doing it
- How it's going to impact everyone

And then, do it again.

I learned this lesson the hard way. A few years ago, I was leading the turnaround of a failing resort. The resort was a mess financially. The team members were disengaged after years of poor leadership and no pay increases. The guest experience had eroded. We knew the team members were the linchpin. If we improved team member engagement, they could create memorable experiences for their guests. That, combined with some much-needed investments in the lodging, would improve guest experiences, prompt return visits, and reverse their sagging finances.

The obvious challenge: How do you re-engage a disillusioned team, even as you're cutting back their hours to save precious cash? Every week and even every day, we communicated to our leadership team the need to engage our full team in the effort. We thought we were doing a good job getting the word out.

Then, one morning I was walking through our offices and one of our sales team members shouted at me as I passed her office, "Hey, GM-guy, it's not working." What's not working? "The people on the team don't get it. They don't understand why we're doing what we're doing. They're frustrated about their pay, and the cutbacks in hours." To which I responded, "Yeah, but we discuss it in all of our daily and weekly leadership meetings. I don't understand why they aren't getting it."

To which she responded, "I don't either. But they're not getting it. So, you need to figure out something else to do about it."

Then came the realization, "Damn. *I* am the Marshmallow Layer." Or, at least, I was allowing it to perpetuate. To remedy that, I started visiting every work team every month. All 1,200 team members on all three shifts.

I toted an easel pad to every session with the current month's financial results, the positive and negative comments we were hearing from guests, and any other specific issues we were grappling with. I wanted them to see exactly the same thing we were seeing at the leadership level and asked for their help in improving the results.

We were very clear. There were a lot of things we could do to improve our finances and the guest experience, but they – the restaurant servers, house-keeping, front desk staff, and recreation staff – had way more impact on the guests than leaders ever could. As guest feedback became more positive and finances began to improve, I wanted them to see the effect they were having.

Perhaps more importantly, those visits enabled me to hear directly from the team members about challenges they were facing. Every month I captured their issues on the easel pad. We used their feedback to knock out the barriers and challenges in their way. We couldn't fix them all. Everyone wanted a pay raise. Everyone had earned a pay raise. But at that point, raising hourly wages would have driven the company into bankruptcy faster. I was brutally honest about that. But there were many things we could fix that made it easier for our team to deliver the best possible guest experience.

It took a huge amount of effort. And the results weren't instantaneous. But the constant rhythm of regular, two-way communications about where we were as an organization and what was and wasn't working helped re-engage our team in the effort to deliver the best possible guest experience. That, in turn, helped us get the results back on the right path.

SETTING THE FOUNDATION FOR A CULTURE OF COMMUNICATIONS: INTEGRITY, TRUST, AND RESPECT

Every time we've seen a high communication environment, we've noticed that everyone in the organization shares a set of common values. Those values are often strikingly similar and simple, starting with a foundation of care, trust, and respect.

In high communication cultures, leaders truly and deeply care about the people in the organization. The leaders want to hear what they have to say about what's working, what's not working, what needs to be changed.

Trust is an absolute requirement to creating the kinds of environments in which people can hold tough conversations (more on these later in this chapter), provide open and honest feedback, or challenge each other in the pursuit of the best ways to execute. Team members must trust their leaders.

You can't create trust overnight; trust requires a track record. I only truly trust by looking in the rear-view mirror. Has what you told me in the past turned out to be true? Did you honor the commitments you made? If you said we were going to make changes, did those changes happen?

It's hard to build a culture of caring and trust without a deep respect of the differences of everyone in the organization. That respect drives the ability to listen and hear at a deep level:

> You can't create trust overnight; trust requires a track record.
>
> - What's the question behind the question?
> - What's the unspoken point?
> - Why is your point of view different from mine?
> - What can I learn from others with different backgrounds and experiences that might help shape my thinking?

In many organizations, leaders guard information on a "need to know" basis. They don't trust their people to handle the information properly. While there are times when sensitive information can't be shared, team members in a culture based on trust will ask a very different question when new information presents itself: Who *else* needs to know? They're thinking about sharing information with as many people as possible, who can then contribute toward making the most effective decisions.

Building a culture of communications through trust requires patience. It takes longer to listen in depth to the listener's ideas and questions – and respond to those ideas and questions – than to bark an order.

In an organization without trust, good news travels faster than bad. Everyone wants to celebrate the good stuff. Bad news flows slower.

It's tough to admit that something isn't going well, and in a low-trust environment, workers immediately turn their attention to, "Who's going to get blamed for this?"

Leaders sometimes have negative reactions to bad news, which only dampens the desire for people to share it. (The old Ryder Truck saying applies: "Don't shoot the messenger; shoot the person who shoots the messenger.") But it's impossible to make the most effective decisions at any level of the organization if people don't have a full set of information to deal with. We'll discuss this topic in more detail in the Visible Scorecards chapter.

THE PHIL AND WILLIE SHOW: HOW TO SQUASH OPEN COMMUNICATIONS

A few years ago, we were engaged by an organization in which "communications" was one of the lowest rated items on its biennial employee engagement survey. Leaders were frustrated because communications had been one of the lowest rated items on the previous survey. They felt like they had put a lot of effort into communicating more openly and thoroughly, and yet their score had actually gone down.

So we went beyond the quantitative feedback and interviewed a cross-section of people in the organization to get their perspective. We were curious, in particular, about whether people had noticed the efforts to communicate more openly and, if so, how they reacted.

It turned out that everyone had noticed. The two operations departments comprising two-thirds of the organization's people were led by Phil and Willie (not their real names). Phil and Willie started a monthly "all-hands" meeting specifically to open lines of communication. But team members agreed that what they called the Phil and Willie Show actually squashed communication.

It went back to the first session, nearly two years earlier. Phil and Willie opened the meeting by sharing what was going on in the division. "They got off to a good start," one team member said. "Then, it all quickly went to hell. They opened up the meeting to questions and ideas. One of the other team members asked a question.

Phil responded, 'That's a dumb question. I'm not going to answer that.' That kind of quieted the group. Then, someone else suggested how we might improve something. Willie said, 'We're NOT going to do that!' So, we all learned in the first 20 minutes of the first meeting that the meeting was just for show. They didn't really want to communicate any better. They just wanted to SAY they communicate better."

A cousin of bad news is the dissenting opinion. Do you invite or discourage disagreement? Several years ago, we were working with the leaders of a start-up organization on their vision and strategy. The head of the organization was known for having strong opinions. But he figured out a way to give people license to disagree. At one point in the conversation, he said, "I'm probably going to disagree with myself before I finish this sentence." That was his way of saying, "If I'm going to disagree with myself, it's certainly okay for you to disagree with me." You could see everyone in the group relax, and a great dialogue ensued for the next several hours.

Regardless of your methods, it's critical that you make it okay for people to express different points of view. It's not enough to make it safe to share bad news or alternative opinions. You have to reach out frequently, in whatever ways your people like to hear from you. A leader's intent on creating a culture of communications won't rest if one particular approach (email, town hall, newsletter, one-on-one conversation) doesn't work. She will experiment until she finds what does work, because she knows it's that important.

I sat next to a sales manager on a flight a few years ago. Her team covered a broad spectrum of generations, from a millennial new to her company, to a few team members who were in their 30s and 40s, and, finally, to the veteran in the group who was in his early 60s.

Spanning those generations created some communication challenges for her. The vet was very comfortable sending and receiving information by fax. The 30- and 40-year-olds liked email. The 20-something was more comfortable with text messages and thought the fax machine should be in a museum. I suggested that must be a challenge to communicate in so many different ways. "Not really," she said. "I have to stay connected with them. If that means I have to communicate with them in three different ways because that's what works, then so be it. I just need to meet them where they are."

Building the necessary trust is the most important and most difficult part of creating a culture of communications. But you can also practice a few techniques that, when used frequently and consistently, send a clear message that you value communications.

Two Up and Two Down: At every level of the organization, people communicate at least two levels up and two levels down. It creates a "closed loop" for communications. Let's say I'm the general manager of a company division – I make it a habit to connect with the leaders two levels below me. I will quickly find out if what I'm communicating is reaching them; and, if what they are trying to communicate makes it to me. If you do that at every level of the organization, you are consistently ensuring that information is punching through the Marshmallow Layer.

Weekly or Daily Stand-Up Meetings: Robust communication cultures always have some sort of regular touch points. They might be daily, weekly, or bi-weekly (less frequent tends to be less effective) to check in on priorities, progress, and to ensure alignment.

In a frontline production or service environment, this might be a 10- to 15-minute stand-up meeting at the beginning of each shift or workday. It might be a weekly leadership team meeting or a weekly or monthly executive team meeting.

Meetings don't have to last forever, and the fewer PowerPoint slides the better. Cover the priorities, what's working well; what's not working well; and potential roadblocks. Invite questions. And you're done. In 10–15 minutes you've aligned every one, so they focus on the key priorities and contribute their best.

MBWA (Management by Wandering Around): Leaders at Hewlett-Packard practiced this in the 1970s. Tom Peters and Bob Waterman popularized the concept in *In Search of Excellence*[1] in 1982. It's at least as valuable today as it was then. Leaders need to be directly in touch with their teams in their work places to build the kind of rapport they need and to truly understand the challenges their team members face. It's an indictment of an organization when we hear, "I never see my manager or my supervisor because they are always tied up in meetings."

---

[1] *In Search of Excellence*, Thomas J. Peters and Robert H. Waterman, Harper and Row, New York, 1982.

Admittedly, since so much more work is done virtually and remotely today than in the 1980s, MBWA might look a little different. But we can use technology – Skype is great, teleconferencing is good, email is neither – to truly connect with people working remotely around the world.

Nucor's Avenue of Appeal is one of the greatest mechanisms we've seen for punching through the Marshmallow Layer and creating a culture of communications. It was one of the four Employee Relations Principles that Ken Iverson established when he transformed the Nuclear Corporation of America in 1965 into what would become the largest steel producer in the United States.

Iverson's premise was that everyone in the company has the right to appeal a decision all the way to the top of an organization, as long as they start with their supervisor and work their way up. In those days, the company was only a few hundred people, so it was easy for employees to exercise their right. Now, with 26,000 team members spread over much of North America and beyond, it's a little harder. Yet it's not unheard of for employees to drive from wherever they work to the corporate office and ask to see the CEO. And when they show up at the reception desk, they are always granted time with the CEO or – if the CEO is away – the most senior executive in the office that day.

ENGAGING IN THE CONVERSATION

One afternoon, some years back, I was imparting some seriously good "Dad Wisdom" to my then 14-year-old daughter. After a few minutes, it was clear to me that she wasn't picking up what I was laying down. I called her out on it and said, "It doesn't seem like you're listening." To which she responded, "Oh, Dad, I'm listening, I'm just not processing."

"Listening, not processing" describes a critical communication breakdown we see throughout many organizations. We know we're supposed to listen. Often, we even have the outward appearances of listening down pat – maintaining eye contact, leaning into the conversation, asking pertinent questions, and paraphrasing the other party's words.

But we're not processing. We might be filtering or preparing our response. We might be multi-tasking (you don't really think you can do that right?), thinking about, or even doing something else mid-conversation.

For whatever reason, we're missing the true meaning of what the person is trying to say, or the feeling behind their words, or the question behind the question they are asking us.

True, effective listening requires fully engaging in the conversation – mind, body, and soul. Individuals and organizations that are successful at fully engaging in conversations tend to follow these basic three steps:

1. Open the Door

> "When I ask you good questions, I want good answers."

Start by making it clear to people that you expect open, honest information to flow. The CEO of a Fortune 500 company made this very clear to me one day early in my relationship with his company. I was in the corporate headquarters working on a project when I crossed paths with him in the breakroom. (Interestingly, and not coincidentally, he'd just finished brewing a pot of coffee.) We had met very casually once before, so when he asked me the standard question, "How are things?" I gave him the standard, and what I thought was socially appropriate answer, "Fine." He then proceeded to practically start thumping me in the chest with his index finger as he said, "Look, I can get that answer from anyone on this floor. Everybody wants to tell me 'fine.' You're from the outside. You have a different perspective. When I ask you good questions, I want good answers."

I got it. Filed away forever. He wanted open, honest thoughts, not candy-coating. Also, not coincidentally, people often told me stories of when the CEO had been previously running a division within the company and had insisted that everyone eat lunch in the division cafeteria every day. As people told me, "The food was horrible. But, every day at lunch we all sat across the table from each other – salespeople, our production team, finance, and accounting. If a salesperson had a customer in for a visit, they had to bring the customer. Making our customers eat that food was torture. But that broke down a lot of walls. Everyone talked to everyone every day. Forcing everyone to eat in the cafeteria also made sure that we communicated with each other."

2. Listen with Empathy

The best listeners use both ears, both eyes, and their hearts. They truly want to understand not only the facts but also the emotion behind what people are sharing – the question behind the question or the issue behind the issue.

But deeply listening is difficult and requires patience and practice. As one leader told us after a deep listening practice session a few years ago, "That was hard, but really worth it."

When we followed up and asked his practice partner how the experience was, she remarked, "It was incredible to have someone suspend judgment and truly just listen."

Here's why deep listening can be difficult (see Figure 4.1).

In every communications process, there is a sender, a message, and a receiver. It seems pretty straightforward, right? The sender gives information to the receiver. The receiver receives it and, boom, they are both on the proverbial "same page."

Unfortunately, it's just not that simple. Both the sender and the receiver are operating with their own unique set of filters. The sender encodes her message based on assumptions she makes about the message and the receiver, which might not be correct. The receiver then decodes the message based upon his own filters, which might misread the sender's intent. In short, there's a lot of static on the line that can lead to misunderstanding.

FIGURE 4.1
The communications process.

A few years ago, we were speaking with an engineer on a construction design and development team. This engineer was distraught. His manager was constantly "beating him up" – challenging him to do more and riding him. "I'm not sure how much more I can take," the engineer told us. "I've got a job offer, and I'm thinking about taking it."

We then talked to the manager. Because our conversations were confidential, we couldn't reveal what the engineer told us. But in the course of the conversation, the manager brought up the same engineer. "I love that guy," he said. "I can always count on him to get the job done. He's my thoroughbred. He's the guy I go to all the time when we have to get things done!"

Clearly, the manager was encoding and delivering a very different message than the one the engineer was receiving.

So how do we make sure we get our signals straight?

- Understand that everyone filters information in different ways.
- Always remember that just because you know the message you wanted to send, that doesn't mean your teammate heard it that way.
- Conversely, the message you received might not be the message your teammate intended to send.
- Listen for the question behind the question or the issue behind the issue. What part of the sender's intended message might be unspoken?
- When you're the sender, ask the receiver to confirm what she heard in her own words.
- When you're the receiver, confirm what you heard in your own words.

3. Create a Closed Loop

Team projects are often undermined by a fatal flaw: People meet, agree to take action, and then … whatever they agreed to dies on the vine.

The final part of engaging in a conversation is following through (a subject so important that Chapter 8 is devoted to it). When it comes to communications, creating a closed loop can help ensure successful follow-through. Creating a closed loop is the best way to make sure that what you said was what they heard.

A few of the best practices we've seen that help create closed loops, in addition to the two up/two down communications we mentioned earlier, include:

Make "Hearing" Visual: Tools like Kanban boards used in Lean processes and Scrum boards used in Agile development allow you to see issues that surface visually. In John Coleman's "Unicorn" organization at FedEx Supply Chain, each workstation had visual Kanban boards on which anyone could post issues as they came up or suggestions for improvement. Leaders reviewed the ideas on the board on a daily or weekly basis with the team in each work cell. They made decisions on the spot about how to deal with each item. Typically, they chose to either implement immediately or study an item for its impact on the rest of the organization or process flow. Rarely would an item get rejected out of hand.

By responding quickly to every suggestion, leadership showed team members that their points of view really did count. When teammates saw that their ideas mattered, they were motivated to suggest more ideas – a positive reinforcing loop.

This approach differs dramatically than the approach symbolized by the dusty, underutilized "Suggestion Boxes" we've seen in many organizations. In those organizations, people drop suggestions in the boxes where they are then evaluated and prioritized at random by unseen forces. Those who made the suggestions receive no feedback about their ideas and rarely see anything implemented. And often what does get implemented is so delayed in time that the person who originally submitted the suggestion either forgot about it or no longer recognizes it as their idea. Suggestions like this typically fall into a metaphorical black hole. Is it any wonder then that people quickly stop submitting suggestions, those boxes gather dust (or used chewing gum), and people feel like they have no avenues for input?

Running Action Lists: We've all been in meetings where good ideas are proposed but go nowhere because no one was held accountable for following up. Running action lists combat this tendency by keeping track of what the team agreed to, who is responsible for taking action, and when the action will be completed.

In some cases, one team member will own the responsibility of taking the list and following up with other team members on the appropriate date.

Or the team can pull out the running action list at the beginning of each team meeting to review each item. The mere act of consistently and publicly tracking each item dramatically improves the probability that the team will resolve it.

As progress is made, completed items are moved to the end of the document to serve as an ongoing reminder of the work the team has completed.

Ask One More Question: Finally, to ensure there is a truly closed loop, the best communicators we know make it a habit to "ask one more question" at the end of a conversation. Asking one more question challenges the assumption that you know all that the other party is trying to share with you. Try to make it an open-ended question, such as:

- Is there anything else we need to talk about?
- What else do I need to know to make the best decision I can?
- What do you know that would be valuable for me to know?

FEEDBACK IS THE BREAKFAST OF CHAMPIONS ... AS LONG AS YOU'RE WILLING TO EAT IT

> *Feedback is the Breakfast of Champions.*
> – Rick Tate
> *Feedback is the Breakfast of Champions ... as long as you're willing to eat it.*
> – Sean Ryan

Feedback doesn't feed if it's not on the menu. Dozens of times over the years we've asked individuals or groups to tell us, "How do you know when you're doing a good job?"

The number one answer is, "I must be doing okay, because no one is telling me that I'm not."

Heck, it even happens to us. A few years ago, we were engaged by a client to build a significant piece of curriculum for their organization. We delivered what we thought was an excellent piece of training, on time, and well within the budget. Then we heard ... nothing. Not a peep. So, our assumption was, "Huh! Hope they liked it. Maybe it was okay. Wonder if/where we screwed up."

A few weeks later, we talked to a person who worked directly for the client who engaged us. I just happened to casually mention this work we had done and that I hadn't heard any feedback from his manager about it. The person we were talking to said, "Oh, he told me, 'It's freaking awesome!'"

Good to know!

There is a significant human cost to not providing the feedback your people need to grow to their fullest potential.

Let me share one story – of hundreds – that puts a spotlight on this issue.

We were working with the senior leadership group in a unit of a multi-national firm. The group included one leader (let's call him Frank) who had been identified by his manager, the VP leading the division, as having the potential to be promoted. Several of the VP's peers had concerns about Frank's potential but were generally not close enough to the situation to have a definitive point of view.

Over the course of our discussion with the leadership group that day, I began to understand why people were hesitant about Frank's potential. It was clear that Frank was a good person – he had a good value set, he truly cared about the organization and his team, and he was technically competent. But it was also clear, from both what he said and what others in the room said, that he had difficulty with Follow-up/Follow-through and creating accountability with both his team and others he worked with.

To his credit, at the end of our session, Frank very pointedly asked for my feedback about him. I said I had some thoughts and offered to discuss it with him in private. He insisted, though, on hearing it in front of the group. While I thought that was risky, I felt compelled to share my observations.

So, I told him: "From our conversation today, your colleagues believe you don't hold your team members accountable. You seem to do a fine job of identifying issues, but you don't provide the tough feedback people need and then follow through to make sure they get corrected."

Fortunately, Frank took the feedback well and agreed with the assessment.

But here's the punch line: After our session, we had the opportunity to tour the unit's operations. Three times during that one-hour tour, Frank pulled me aside to thank me for the direct, honest feedback I provided him. He said, "No one – including my boss – has ever provided me with that kind of feedback."

To emphasize the point: His manager, who wanted him to succeed and was actively campaigning for Frank to be promoted, had never given him the very feedback he needed to succeed.

Frank was willing to eat the breakfast of champions, but no one was willing to feed it to him.

What's the Cost of Not Providing the Feedback People Need?

To Frank: The sad result was that it likely had prevented him from being promoted for several years. His boss had withheld valuable information from him, information that might have cost him opportunities to advance in the company.

To Frank's team: What growth opportunities had they missed because of Frank not holding them accountable for being their best?

To Frank's business unit: How much could performance have improved if Frank had been more effective with Follow-up/Follow-through and holding people accountable?

To the larger organization: Frank's company had a need for a steady pipeline of talent to fuel its growth and continuing success. What was the cost of Frank not growing to the extent of his potential to enable him to move up in the organization?

What's the cumulative cost of dozens of Franks being held back because they are not growing and developing as much as they could?

Providing Effective Feedback

Here are a few general principles about providing the kind of feedback people need to be fed the "breakfast of champions."

- More is better. Operate on the assumption that you're not giving people enough. Just give more.
- Different people take feedback different ways. Customize your efforts to the person and the situation. My daughter was around 4, taking her first set of swimming lessons, when she taught me this. I was a relatively new and young manager at that time and I had been taught the classic Dale Carnegie approach of being "Hearty with your approbation." That's a big word, but I took it to mean "celebrate successes in public and make it loud!" One night at swim class, my

daughter swam the full way across the pool for the first time. That seemed like something that should be celebrated loudly ... really loudly. So, in a moment of incredibly bad parenting, I started jumping up and down and cheering her for crossing the pool. She briefly looked at me and then burst out crying. After swim class ended, as we walked to the car, she gritted her teeth and said, "Don't ever do that to me again!"

My younger son, on the other hand, gets fired up by that kind of feedback. He would be ecstatic that mom or dad was celebrating his success that way.

Different people and different situations call for providing positive feedback in different ways. (Providing constructive feedback in private is almost always the better course of action.) Some like it loud and boisterous; for others, a quiet "thumbs-up" is sufficient. Either way, more frequent is critical.

COURAGEOUS COMMUNICATIONS

Now we come to the acid test. If you religiously pursue the previous four elements above, your organization will conduct communications more effectively than most. You'll master the mechanics of communications, and that, by itself, will drastically reduce the misunderstandings and confusion that plague so many organizations without communications discipline.

But there's no getting around it: If you're not prepared to suck it up and engage in personal, one-on-one conversations that confront important problems, you're limiting the potential growth of your people and your organization.

Conflict is all around us. People have different perspectives on how to solve a problem or even what the problem is. They have different perspectives on goals and objectives and the best way to accomplish them. Leaders and their teams have different perspectives on performance and how well people are supported.

Creating an environment for healthy conflict is critical to creating a culture of caring, trust, and respect. How leaders resolve conflicts is one of the key indicators of their overall effectiveness as leaders. Organizations that relish healthy conflict and deal with it in positive ways tend to out-perform those that shun conflict or believe that conflict and disagreement are bad.

Well-managed conflict isn't bad. In fact, it's imperative in any organization striving for growth. A healthy, growing organization is always trying something new, and people are going to disagree about whether that new thing is a good idea.

Employees consistently rate "communications" near the bottom in their company surveys. What are they complaining about? Trust me, they're not asking for more newsletters or tweets. Most of the time, they mean: "We got stuff we need to talk about in this organization that we're not talking about. And, frankly, if you're a senior leader, you often don't even know we're not talking about it."

"I'm Only Telling You This Because I'm Leaving the Company"

Stifling the tough conversations has a debilitating effect on organizations. I was once working with several levels of leadership – about 35 people – in a division of a manufacturing company. Our objective was to identify and eliminate roadblocks to more effective execution. We held a series of breakout sessions to get everyone engaged in the conversation.

After one round of breakouts, the groups were asked to share what they had come up with. A frontline supervisor in one of the groups, let's call him Bob, brought up an issue that, while critical, was resolved adeptly in about five minutes of group conversation.

As we were wrapping up that discussion, another person in Bob's breakout group said, "I'd just like to point out that Bob would not have brought that up if he wasn't leaving the company on Friday."

WHAT? Hold the phone. "Let me make sure I understand," I said. "Bob would not have brought up a relatively minor issue, that this group just resolved in five minutes, except for the fact that he's leaving the company in a couple of days? I have to know ... why?"

The question was followed by dead silence. Shifting in seats. Careful shoe examinations.

After much digging and prodding, we ended up having an excellent conversation. We took a two-hour side trip into this issue – well worth the time. Most of the group admitted that they didn't feel comfortable addressing issues with their peers or their leaders. The level of trust within the organization was not high enough to support it. It was also obvious that some of them lacked the courage or the skills to address the conflicts they needed to address.

Finally, it became clear that senior leaders in the organization were unaware that people weren't addressing issues that needed to be addressed.

What about the rest of the participants? Well, they were adamant that they didn't have any issues that they had not addressed with others. More on that below.

The Follow-Up

I was back a month later as a follow-up to our initial conversation. A few fascinating facts emerged:

First, it turned out that Bob's issue with communicating with his manager (let's call him Alex) went back more than 20 years to when he and Alex had been peers in another organization. One had turned down an invitation to the other's house for dinner. That was it. The two never talked it out, and the resentment followed them over the years to their new place of employment. Their conflict had, to some extent, infected the entire management team – all because two people had avoided talking about a conflict from more than 20 years earlier.

Second, remember all those people who said in the initial workshop that they didn't have any hidden issues? Every one of them pulled me aside at some point during my visit and copped to the fact that they, too, had issues that they'd had to sort out with one or more of their peers. And they all also talked about how liberating it had been to finally hold those courageous communications and get issues out on the table.

It also became clear that since they couldn't talk about routine issues that the organization typically ate for breakfast, they surely were not talking about far trickier issues around quality, performance, hand-offs between workgroups, etc. By learning how to hold more courageous communications, they quickly evolved to a much more productive culture.

Having worked with thousands of leaders over the years, I can tell you that how they conduct courageous conversations distinguishes average leaders from great leaders.

What's the difference?

The most effective leaders both Think and Act differently about courageous communications than other leaders.

Thinking Differently about Conflict

Many leaders shy away from conflict. They want to be liked and fear that a conversation laced with conflict will erode their likeability. Great leaders think about potential conflict in an entirely different way. Working through conflict is the path to improving the organization and the relationship between two people, and they seek to engage the other side in the journey.

Art Smuck, former CEO of FedEx Supply Chain and one of the best performing senior executives I've had the opportunity to work with, operates by what he describes as the Hippocratic Oath for Leaders: "I mean you no harm." He shares this belief openly with team members and works to make sure they understand he would never purposefully do anything to hurt them. He feels his role as leader is to help the organization and every individual be the best they can be and he makes it clear for all that he is there to support exactly that. His team – including managers, peers, and direct reports – gets direct and tough feedback but always from a caring/trusting perspective. They know he has their best interest, and that of their organization, at heart and that he wants them to strive to realize the potential he knows they are capable of. While the ineffective manager might view tough and caring as conflicting traits, he sees tough as an essential part of caring.

It helps when you start from a solid foundation – the culture of trust, caring, and respect we've talked about. It's no coincidence that organizations that deal with conflict and courageous communications most effectively have higher levels of trust. They treat tough conversations as a natural part of who they are. Since disrespectful behavior isn't tolerated, teammates can start a courageous conversation confident that the outcome will be a path to improvement, not punishment.

Acting Differently

More effective leaders also act differently when dealing with conflict, starting with how they prepare for a courageous communication. They ask three questions:

1. *Does this conflict need to be addressed?*
2. *When do you choose to confront?*
3. *How do we create a safe environment in which to confront the issue?*

Question #1: Does This Conflict Need to Be Addressed?

A colleague of mine once worked for a manager whose catch phrase was, "That's not a battleground we want to die on." The problem was that there were NO battlegrounds he ever wanted to die on or even suffer a minor wound. So the people on his team didn't get the feedback they needed to be their best. They felt unsupported. They weren't held accountable for results. Ultimately, they underperformed, and their customers didn't get the best of what the company could offer.

On the other hand, not every issue needs to be confronted. Early in my career, I worked for one of the worst bosses ever. His catch phrase was, "You just need to go kick more ass," which he did on a regular basis. No issue was too small for him to confront. While he rarely turned his ire – bordering on insanity – toward me, he regularly wore out my peers about trivial details.

As a result, everyone avoided him as much as possible and did what they could to just get by. No one was even close to fully engaged in an effort to drive the division forward.

Question #2: When Do You Choose to Confront?

It's hard to list all the possibilities, but here are a few questions to provide a starting point:

- Is someone behaving outside your organization's values?
- Is performance below acceptable or below what someone is capable of?
- Is someone's behavior disrupting the ability of the team to perform its best?
- How would you feel if a story about the situation appeared on the evening news, or the front page of the newspaper, and you were portrayed as not acting to intercede?

If these questions point you toward confrontation, ask yourself, "What issue do we need to confront?" Focus on the issue that's likely to have the biggest impact.

That issue might change next month. Say someone has shown up late for work a few times recently. You address it with him. He owns his behavior and promises it won't happen again. All good.

Then, two or three weeks later, he shows up late again. What issue do you address?

If you thought, "Talk to him again about being late," raise your hand.

Actually, there is a more important problem. Now it's about his failure to honor his commitment to you – an integrity issue – and not whether he makes it to work on time.

Question #3: How Do We Create a Safe Environment in Which to Confront the Issue?

As noted above, creating a safe environment for courageous communications starts well before the conversation itself. It's difficult to have a truly effective, tough conversation with someone if you haven't built an environment of trust and respect, or if you have no relationship with the other person.

Presuming you've built the proper foundation, establishing a safe environment means finding a place to have the most productive conversation possible. The old adage, "Praise in public, criticize in private" generally holds true. But we also have to make conversations psychologically safe for people. When people feel threatened, we are unlikely to engage them in a fully collaborative conversation. We may get compliance; we'll rarely get collaboration. They need to understand that you have a point of view and they have a point of view. It's not a matter of merely asserting your point of view. It is a matter of both parties learning together and coming to a collective point of view – then mutually agreeing on a course of action for moving forward.

Holding the Courageous Conversation

Several years ago, I was working with two leaders at roughly the same time. They worked for different organizations, but I was struck with how similar they were.

Both had a great sense of the strengths, weaknesses, and potential of their respective organizations. Both had a great feel for their groups' strategy and relative position in the marketplace. Both understood financial issues. Both had earned a great deal of respect from their peers, managers, and direct reports for their intellect, knowledge, and understanding of the business.

They differed in several ways, but one critical aspect really distinguished them: their willingness and ability to carry out courageous conversations.

"Samantha" would initiate the courageous conversation whenever when she saw something that needed to be addressed. She had no problem confronting anyone when it was necessary – boss, peer, or direct report. In every conversation, she made sure they understood her point of view. And (again, when appropriate) she actively sought out their point of view on the conflict rather than dictating her point of view. More on this idea later.

"Dave" took the opposite approach. He was just as perceptive as Samantha, so he knew when he needed to address a problem face to face. But he couldn't bring himself to do it. Worse, in his frustration, he would occasionally discuss the lingering problem with another colleague, not the person who needed the feedback. He simply lacked the courage to confront others directly.

Samantha's career continued to progress. Dave's plateaued.

This is not an isolated case. We have seen dozens of otherwise talented leaders hit the proverbial career ceiling because they lack the confidence and/or the capability to gracefully manage courageous conversations.

If you're not comfortable with courageous conversations, join the club. Most people aren't. Here are a few tips to help you get started.

Frameworks, Not Scripts

First, we don't believe in scripts. Memorizing a few key phrases – whether you're greeting guests in a restaurant or holding a tough conversation with a peer – isn't genuine or effective. Courageous conversations are interactive. They require deep listening to what your conversation partner is saying and feeling and really hearing the message behind their words. If you're working from a script and the other person is not – and he won't be – the conversation will be off-script as soon as the other person starts to talk. Then you'll have the choice of either abandoning your script or lurching back to it, which will require you to ignore what your conversation partner just said to you.

We prefer frameworks and outlines of the key principles that apply. Having a solid framework allows you to fully engage in the rich dialogue that tough conversations require.

So, let's talk about a framework for holding effective courageous communications.

Master the First 30 Seconds

You must get to the point quickly. You're having the conversation because you want one or two specific things to change, and you know how you think they need to change. So say that. Define the problem. Think of the problem as a gap between what is actually happening and what needs to happen. Describe that gap and clearly explain what you believe needs to change. Then, usually, listen to your conversation partner's point of view.

If you stammer, fumble, muddle your words, or are not clear in any way, you leave a lot of room for confusion and misinterpretation. You can make the situation worse, not better. To master those first 30 seconds, you may need to practice what you're going to say. And, sometimes, it makes sense to practice with a practice partner who can give you the feedback you need to make sure your message is completely clear.

What if you have more than one or two specific things that need to change? If that's the case:

- That's a pretty good sign that you've waited too long to hold this conversation, and
- You probably need to have more than one conversation.

If you bring up a laundry list of issues, your co-worker is likely to feel like you're piling on and will respond defensively. Pick one or two issues – perhaps the most critical problem, or maybe start with a problem that's relatively simple to solve so you both can get a "win" under your belts before addressing the next issue – and table the rest.

Don't Sugarcoat or Turn the Conversation into a Compliment Sandwich

A lot of us have been taught the script of "say something positive, give people the critical feedback, and then close the conversation with something else positive." That script is a recipe for communication disasters.

All of us filter information. We tend to filter in information that we're interested in or we like; we tend to filter out information we don't like or find unpleasant. When you feed someone the "compliment sandwich," they tend to hear the positive items at the front and back end of the script and get confused by, or totally miss, the important stuff in the middle.

You're having the conversation because you need to address something important. Starting with language that pretends this isn't serious, or isn't on point, just confuses the person who needs to receive your feedback. Besides, the other person very likely knows you're there to discuss an important problem. If you start the conversation with a compliment, she's just waiting for the shoe to drop.

Engage in Dialogue … Most of the Time. Adapt Accordingly

If this is the first time, you're addressing the issue, you want to check your own thinking and engage in joint problem-solving. Why is there a gap? Does the other person perceive the situation the same way you do? If not, why not? And how will you mutually resolve the situation?

If this is the third time, you're discussing the same issue, you probably don't want to spend much time listening to what your co-worker has to say. At this point, it's probably time to tell her what has to be done and explain the consequences to the organization and to the person if it doesn't happen.

Manage the Conversation within the Conversation

Tough conversations often involve a significant level of emotion for both you and the other person involved. Pretty clearly, you need to keep your emotions in control. Be prepared for a wide range of emotions from the other side. Managing the conversation within the conversation means:

- Deciding if you need to confront any issues or emotional reactions that come up
- Deciding what you're going to confront and what you'll let slide
- Mastering the opening of this side conversation ("Your reaction (anger, yelling, clamming up, etc.) is getting in the way of us having a productive conversation.")
- Resolving that issue (if possible within the conversation)
- Getting back on track with the initial conversation. (Or, making the decision to break off the conversation to let emotions subside, then getting back together at a clearly defined point in the very near future.)

Close Clearly

Make sure there's no confusion about the issue, why it's important, what you're both committing to change, and what your timeframe is to make the change. When will you talk again?

Creating a culture of communications is difficult. As Tom Hanks said to Geena Davis in A League of Their Own, "It's supposed to be difficult. If it was easy everyone could play the game." Unlike professional baseball, however, everyone can play the game of communication. It takes a willingness to focus and energy to execute on the issues outlined in this chapter. When you do, it will create an environment in which people can execute much more effectively, and...

- Everyone is more engaged in their work
- Issues get identified and resolved
- People are both willing and able to address the tough issues which keeps them from getting buried and creating festering wounds within the organization.

THOUGHT STARTER QUESTIONS

1. To what extent does the Marshmallow Layer exist in your organization?
   - What are you doing, or can you do, to remove it?
2. How do people assess the overall level of communications in your organization? Why? What needs to change? What's the level of trust within your organization? How do you know? Are you sure?
3. To what extent are you holding all the courageous conversations you need to be holding with others?
   - What forces enable your organization to deal with healthy conflict?
   - What forces are blocking courageous communications from happening?
   - How well have you created an environment in which difficult communications can take place?
   - How willing and able are people to hold the courageous communications that are necessary?

4. How well have you handled the tough conversations you've had with others?

5. Do you have mechanisms in place to ensure that if there is an issue with communications people have an outlet to bypass the blockage?

6. Are you willing to feed people the tough feedback they need to be their best?

7. Are you willing to "eat the breakfast" that others are trying to feed you?

FIRST STEPS

Warning: Some of these actions might freak other people out.

1. Go slowly, but don't be afraid. Identify a situation in which a courageous conversation hasn't gone as ideally as it could: either you've avoided it, not accomplished what you needed to accomplish, or, even, over-asserted yourself. Think through how that conversation should have been resolved. What would you do differently? Practice first, if necessary. Then, go hold the conversation or hold it again if you've already tried and it didn't go well.

2. Find an opportunity to practice closed-loop communications. Start a two up/two down process or assess the level of communications in your organization. Are people truly hearing and processing the messages you're trying to send? Are you truly hearing and processing the messages people are trying to share with you?

3. Practice truly engaging in a conversation with a peer or someone on your team. Seek to fully understand their point of view. Listen freely without judging or thinking about your response. Afterwards, reflect on the conversation. How different did it feel? To what extent did the other person respond differently?

4. Find someone who needs the feedback you could provide – a team member, peer, or manager. Then go provide it.

5

SET Result-Oriented Goals: Aligning Results to Strategy

Several years ago, we were working with a major telecommunications company which had a strategic objective of improving its customer loyalty. We spent a few days assessing the organization, focusing on one of the organization's call centers. The customer service reps had been given a goal of "handling 100 calls per day." While the organization did perform customer surveys, feedback was so sporadic that it was hard to get a handle on the qualitative performance of any of the individual reps. The customer service reps were explicitly measured and graded solely on the number of calls they took each day.

At times they would get tied up with customers who had complex problems. Those calls took longer to resolve, which would then cause them to fall short of their daily call goal. They knew from experience that they would get feedback from their managers about coming up short of the goals.

To make up for the shortfall, they would hang up on some customers after about ten seconds – the minimum amount of time for their systems to register that they had taken the call – just to boost their call count. To avoid being completely rude, the reps would pretend they were having connection issues, "Hello, hello? I can't hear you / Sorry, please call back." Then they would hang up. (Let the irony of that seep in … telecommunications company customer service reps faking bad call connections so they could hit their "customer service" goals.)

The goal that was presumably in place to improve the customer experience was, in fact, making it worse. Rather than aligning results to the strategy, the goal was unintentionally misaligning the results to the strategy.

Virtually everyone agrees that (A) goals are important to generating results and (B) that individual and team goals at every level of the organization need alignment to the organization's strategy. Yet when we talk with people about their goals what we find is:

- Performers at any level, from the frontline to senior executives, often do not know what their goals are.
- They are misaligned with what their managers think they ought to be doing, or with the organization's strategy.
- Many times, when people do have goals, those goals describe *the activities they should perform*, rather than the results they should achieve, which can lead to endless activity without meaningful results.

The SET (Start-End-Timeframe) Goals Gear outlines how to set goals that align to the strategy and truly help translate strategy to results. Effective Goals:

1. Are aligned to the strategy.
2. Result-oriented, not activity-based.
3. Defined in SET format.
4. Stretch the organization beyond its current capabilities.

ALIGN GOALS TO THE STRATEGY

There is surely nothing quite so useless as doing with great efficiency what should not be done at all.

> – Peter Drucker, consultant and author known as
> "the founder of modern management"

Goals must be aligned to the strategy. We've seen dozens of situations in which people outline what they think their goals are and put huge effort into executing them only to find that they are not aligned to the organization's strategy. To paraphrase Drucker, they were very aggressively and efficiently being useless! As a result, despite the best of intentions, performance suffers.

A few notable examples:

- In a study we did for an HR department, we found that 60% of the stuff they did was not aligned to the organization's strategy.
- A conversation between a sales manager and a production manager in the same company over dinner with excellent wine one night: Production manager: "Why don't you sell what we have made and put in inventory?" Sales manager: "Why don't you produce what we can sell? The stuff we can sell generates a higher margin than that stuff you have sitting in the warehouse." Both were rigorously executing their goals in isolation from each other and their company's strategy.
- In a different company on a different continent: In an annual business planning session, the production manager said his goal was to increase throughput by 20%–30% in the upcoming year; the sales manager said her goal was to sell a higher percentage of more value-added product, which ran slower through the production process – the opposite of the production manager's goal.
- Several executives at a consumer products company we worked with: They proudly shared the detailed process maps they had built to optimize their operations. We asked them to tell us how those process maps connected to each other. They were dumbfounded by the question: "Well, we never thought about that." They were each optimizing their processes based upon their myopic viewpoint, with no focus on the customers or what created value for their company.

The first issue is to align individual and team goals to the strategy. To create goals that align to your organization's strategy, think about:

- What are the goals of your company or division?
- Then, what are the goals of your department that align with those company or division goals?
- Then, what are the individual or team goals that align with the department and organization goals?

The second part is to align performers and managers at every level of the organization. We've repeated the "5-on-5" exercise described below hundreds of times with individuals and groups over the years, and we consistently get the same results: In the exercise, we ask leaders and performers each to write down a list of the performer's top five goals. How many do you think match?

On average, only two.

That means that team members are aligned with and working on what their bosses think are the highest priorities about 40% of the time ... but 60% of the time they are not. Going way back to Chapter 1, is it any wonder, then, why:

- *Fortune* Magazine said: "...less than 10% of strategies, effectively formulated, are effectively executed."
- *Harvard Business Review* said: "...the prize for closing the strategy-performance gap is huge: increasing performance by at least 50% for most organizations."

PLAYING 5-ON-5: PLEASE DO THIS AT HOME!

Are your goals "mutually agreed upon?"

Ask each of your direct reports to write down what they think their top three to five goals are. Simultaneously, write down what you think the top three to five goals are for each of them. (If you think there are more than five, you haven't identified the most critical ones.)

Then, match the lists. Sit down with each direct report, or even your whole team, and compare the lists. How many match?

Next, align the lists. Make sure there is complete alignment. As you do that, make sure each of the individual and/or team goals are aligned with the strategy and goals of the organization, business unit, and department.

After you get alignment, spend some time discussing why the lists don't match. Get to the root cause of those issues to help avoid future misalignment.

Finally, repeat the process every three to six months. While consistently following the Strategy-Execution-Results (SXR) process should eliminate many causes of misalignment, some misalignment will inevitably creep in. Playing 5-on-5 every few months will catch that before the Goals Gear gets too wobbly.

Just getting aligned correctly on goals – one simple step – should help you achieve much of that 50%!

(See Box: Playing 5-on-5: PLEASE do this at home!)

RESULT-ORIENTED GOALS

Have you ever had days when it felt like you were up to your armpits in activity but, in retrospect, it didn't feel like you got much *done*?

There are other causes for this, which we'll discuss later. But often it's because your goals, even if they are aligned with your organization's strategy, are defined in terms of activities (stuff to DO) rather than results (what you need to ACHIEVE).

Customer service rep: Answer 100 calls per day.
Salesperson: Make 25 sales calls per day.
In our personal lives: Eat better and floss daily.

We often ask the wait staff in restaurants to tell us what their goals are. They commonly list the *activities* they do:

Wait tables.
Take orders.
Turn the tables quickly.
Be courteous and responsive to the guests.

All of these are critical *activities*.

Yet, when we ask the restaurant managers what their goals are for the wait staff, it is almost always "Increase profits for the restaurant," a critical *result*.

Result-Oriented Goals change the game. They define what the performer must *accomplish* rather than what he/she should *do*.

The customer service rep's Result-Oriented Goals might be to improve customer loyalty or customer retention.
The sales rep's Result-Oriented Goals might be to increase sales volume, gross margin or share of wallet with target customers.

In our personal lives, our goals might be to get the dental hygienist to stop dogging us about the fact that we don't floss often enough!

In each of those cases, do the performers still have to do certain activities? Of course. But *now the performer owns the result* and the responsibility to identify and act on the highest-impact activities (what we call Performance Drivers, see Chapter 7) that achieve the result. The actions she takes have a crisp, clear purpose: Hit the goal.

The restaurant server must learn which activities generate the best profits for the restaurant (hint: sell drinks and desserts) while effectively serving the guests so they return.

The customer service rep still takes phone calls, but now it's his responsibility to handle the calls in a way that builds customer loyalty.

The salesperson still makes sales calls. But it's up to her to target the customers or products that increase volume, gross margin or share of wallet.

In our personal lives:

To hit our weight, strength, or body composition goal, we still must exercise. But we can adjust the exercise to the type, timing, and duration that best allows us to hit the goal. Having the Result-Oriented Goals creates intent and purpose. It decreases the chances that we're just going through the motions.

And, sorry, you still have to floss more often.

SET (START-END-TIMEFRAME) GOALS

Once you've identified the result, the next step is to refine the goals to SET form.

- Starting point.
- Ending point.
- Timeframe for achievement.

We use the acronym SET to describe these effective, Result-Oriented Goals.

The starting point and ending point define the gap between your current results and where you want to be. We have found time and again that merely understanding this gap drives performance. It also can engage everyone in the organization to close the gap and to bring all their creativity and energy to the effort. In The Fifth Discipline,[1] Peter Senge talks about the principle of creative tension, which is the stress people feel when there is a gap between an organization's vision and its current reality. Defining the start and end point for goals creates the same kind of tension, but the tension is focused on the goal. The only way to release the tension is to either achieve the goal or change the goal.

Leaders must first define the gap – and then engage their team in the journey to close the gap. Interestingly, in most cases, the more difficult point to understand is often the start. We're amazed at the number of people we've worked with who have a clear picture of where they want to go in performance terms but little idea of where they are.

Compound this lack of awareness with activity-based goals, and it's no wonder that most people are just going through the motions, completely lacking intent or focus. As soon as they understand the gap, they get energized to close it. If we then give them the latitude to be creative and own how they close the gap, we begin to fully engage them in the effort and create organizations where everyone can be their best.

Remember the resort we discussed earlier in Chapter 4? This was a perfect example of how defining the gap can turn a business around. When we came on the scene the resort was running out of cash and very near bankruptcy. Guests were aggravated by poor sleep experiences and run-down amenities. After years of flat pay and misaligned leadership, team members were dispirited.

We knew that one key to a successful turnaround was to re-engage the team. They seemed engaged with only one question: "When am I going to get a pay raise?" The answer – "Not anytime soon given our cash position" – wasn't going to satisfy anyone.

To help them better understand our direction, and why we couldn't give them pay raises, we defined the gap for them. We showed them the cash position and our monthly burn rate. I told them, "We can give you a raise tomorrow, but without improving the guests' experience and bringing them back, all that does is cause us to go bankrupt and close sooner."

---

[1] *The Fifth Discipline*, Peter Senge, Doubleday, 1990, pp. 150 151.

Our nearly 1,200 team members quickly understood the gravity of the situation.

Then we made the tough ask: "Look, the only way we're successful is for all of us to figure out a way to deliver a great guest experience and get them to come back. We need you, in spite of no raises for the last three years and no possibility of a raise in the foreseeable future, to wow the guests. Get them to want to be here. That will turn cashflow positive. Then, we can figure out how to compensate you better."

While we changed a lot of other things working through the turnaround, that conversation and the ones that followed were instrumental in engaging the team and unleashing their abilities and creativity to help us solve the problem.

Merely defining the gap was critical to our ultimate success. (And, it took awhile, but the team members eventually reaped the rewards of

WHY SET RESULT-ORIENTED GOALS ARE SMARTER THAN SMART GOALS

Many people reading this book will be familiar with the concept of SMART goals, which traces back to a 1981 Management Review article by George Duran. SMART stands for specific, measurable, achievable, relevant, and time-bound. SMART goals gained currency as part of the popularity of the management-by-objectives concept created by Peter Drucker.

While we think that SMART goals can be helpful in a lot of situations, we think SET goals are even smarter. Let's look at each part of SMART goals to see why:

SPECIFIC

Goals *do* need to be specific. Many managers are ineffective because they don't make their goals specific enough. Or in other situations, they make them too specific and stifle the creativity of their team.

For example, the same specific goal that provides critical guidance to the new employee is demotivating micromanagement for a veteran top performer. One size doesn't fit all. Imagine telling your 20-year-old son, on leave from the Army, "Clean your room." That's all the instruction he needs. He has been professionally trained by the U.S. Army to clean a room. Now go tell his 10-year-old brother, "Clean your room," with no further instruction. Good luck with that.

A specific goal is helpful, but it's only the start. You need to provide the right level of detail for each member of your team.

MEASURABLE

We agree goals should be measurable. We've dedicated the whole next chapter to building Visible Scorecards to ensure performance versus the goals you set are measurable and trackable.

ACHIEVABLE

You might think ensuring that a goal is achievable makes sense. Usually, it is. What's the point in creating a goal that your team can't achieve? But as we outlined in the section on Stretch Goals, organizations need to set goals that occasionally appear to be unachievable. That forces the organization to challenge its underlying thinking and mental models to disrupt itself before an outside competitor can do so. An organization that focuses entirely on achievable goals might miss a critical chance to transform itself.

RELEVANT

In the SXR Framework, "relevant" is redundant. If you're following the SXR model, you're already asking yourself the critical questions to tie your goals directly to your organization's strategy. The goals you set are, by design, relevant.

TIME-BOUND

In the SET Goals framework, "T" for time-bound is a given.

their efforts. More guests meant more hours of work which increased their pay. Then, the resort was eventually able to increase their hourly rate, too.)

Defining the start and end point for goals generates the creative tension necessary to close the gap. Timeframe puts energy into achieving the goal. As many business gurus and leaders have noted, a goal without a deadline is just a dream.

Establishing a timeframe for goal achievement focuses attention and energy. Virtually everyone has experienced the energy that goes into completing a school or work project on deadline. Adding the Timeframe step to Result-Oriented Goals creates the same kind of energy.

Timeframe also allows people to manage their time and priorities. We were talking to a sales rep a few years ago about his monthly sales goal. His company had just instituted a new sales goal system. Previously, their goals had been ambiguous and discretionary. With the new goal system, he had monthly targets he was supposed to hit for sales volume. It was relatively late in the month and he was short of his target. It was late in the afternoon, about the time that he previously would have headed for home. Our conversation was short. We asked him about his goals. He took one look at his tracking system and said, "Dude, I'd love to chat with you. But it's not like the old days. I'm short of my target this month. I've got a couple hours left in which I can call customers, so I can hit the target."

Here are a few examples of SET Result-Oriented Goals:

For a production team or team member in a business where volume is critical, a SET goal might be: Increase productivity from five units per hour (Starting point) to eight units per hour (Ending point) over the next two months (Timeframe).

For a sales team, a SET goal might be: Increase market share in the agricultural vertical market from 15% (Starting point) to 20% (Ending point) within the next 12 months (Timeframe).

For a salesperson, her primary SET goal might be: Increase sales in my territory from 100,000 units to 150,000 units by the end of this year.

For a quality representative, a SET goal might be: Reduce quality defects from 1% to 0.1% over the next two years.

If you are in a leadership position, it is a good idea to actively involve your team members in setting Result-Oriented Goals. People like knowing that what they do matters!

Quantitative Versus Qualitative Goals

It's probably obvious that we are big fans of quantitative goals. We're hardly alone. Quantitative goals allow you to keep score and performers to understand how much progress they are making. In turn, this generally increases the ownership people feel for the results they deliver.

There are, however, many situations in which goals can only be addressed qualitatively, such as customer service, how engaging the culture of the organization is, and the effectiveness of leaders at engaging people.

While there can be some quantitative aspects to those items (on-time delivery as a contributor-to-customer satisfaction, surveys to measure customer loyalty), many items are better measured qualitatively rather than quantitatively. In most cases, the key question is "Qualitative from whose perspective?"

For customer satisfaction or loyalty, the answer is obvious: Customers.
For how engaging the culture is: The team members.
For the qualitative components of leadership: Those being led.

Once you've decided where you need to set a goal, say, overall customer satisfaction, and who's got the data (the customers), then you can use the SET approach to define the gap and create energy around closing it. For example:

Increase the Net Promoter Score, a critical measure of customer loyalty, from 65% to 75% by the end of this year.

Playing within the Values of the Organization

As we discussed in Chapter 3, the culture of the organization needs to align with the strategy to enable you to attract, retain, and unleash the full capabilities of people in your organization. Behaving within the value set of an organization is not easily captured quantitatively. Nonetheless, you can establish descriptors of behavior that help define expectations and outline which behaviors fall inside and outside the boundaries.

Done or Not Done

Other goals fall into the category of either "done" or "not done." (For instance, organizations that install new Enterprise Resource Planning (ERP) systems or human capital management systems.) The Result-Oriented Goal is "done and operating according to specifications." Those specifications define what "done" means. The project plans contain multiple milestones, scheduled dates, and budget objectives. But, the Result-Oriented Goal is get it installed and operating effectively by July 1 of next year.

So, challenge yourselves to find the quantifiable goal, but know that at the end of the day, some goals are best expressed without a number.

STRETCH GOALS

Many years ago, I drove a Volkswagen Jetta. I had a colleague who drove a Porsche 911. One afternoon, on an empty freeway east of Bakersfield, California, Fred and I were tooling around in his Porsche. He hit the accelerator on the on-ramp and we went from 0 to 105 mph in what seemed like an instant.

That night driving home, I tried to replicate that performance in my Jetta. It became clear very quickly that, no matter how smoothly I shifted or how hard I pushed on the accelerator, I was not going to get to 105 mph as quickly as Fred in his Porsche.

If you have a Volkswagen and you want to make it go as fast as a Porsche, what do you do? Well, you obviously don't get there by merely pushing on the accelerator harder...

...you have to redesign the car – different engine, transmission, clutch, steering. You might even want to redesign the brakes since they will be under much more stress.

That's the purpose of stretch goals – they force you to fundamentally redesign the car (the systems, structures, processes, and people capabilities and practices) to achieve dramatically higher levels of performance – or a different kind of performance completely.

In May 1961, U.S. President John F. Kennedy said in a speech to Congress, "First, I believe that this nation should commit itself to achieving the goal, before this decade is out, of landing a man on the moon and returning him safely to the Earth.[2]"

President Kennedy's speech outlined the ultimate stretch goal: organize the resources of the country to put a man on the moon and return him

---

[2] John F. Kennedy, Speech to Congress, May 25, 1961.

safely in less than ten years, starting from far behind the Soviet Union in what was then called the Space Race.

Showing an intuitive grasp of the value of SET goals, Kennedy also said in the speech, "I believe we possess all the resources and talents necessary. But the facts of the matter are that we have never made the national decisions or marshaled the national resources required for such leadership. We have never specified long-range goals on an urgent time schedule or managed our resources and our time so as to ensure their fulfillment."

Stretch goals aren't looking for 10% improvement; they're about ten times improvement. To achieve these outrageous results, they challenge your organization's systems and mental models, driving you to innovate. They demolish current thinking, motivate action, and challenge everyone to change everything except the organization's core values and principles. You're not going to get there by doing everything the same way, only a little better. You're going to get there by discovering a new way.

When setting goals, people usually anchor their expectations to current levels of performance and what they think is possible. Until the 1950s, people thought it was impossible for a human to run a mile in less than four minutes. Then, in 1954, Roger Bannister ran a mile in 3:59.4. Within three years – *16 other runners* also cracked the four-minute barrier.

What happened to the barrier that prevented humans from running the four-minute mile? Was there a sudden leap in human evolution?

No. It was a shift in mental models. Once Bannister showed that breaking a four-minute mile was possible, other people also believed a four-minute mile was possible. Other athletes reset their performance goals and achieved significantly greater results.

Stretch goals require the organization to envision what's possible rather than merely attempt incremental improvement. The disruptors – Amazon's goal to sell everything to everyone or Uber and Lyft reinventing taxi service – challenge the fundamental underlying assumptions of whole industries. Well-set stretch goals force the organization to disrupt itself.

Getting Comfortable with Being Uncomfortable

When you set stretch goals, many people will likely be uncomfortable and want to go back to the old way. Mistakes will be made as individuals and the organization work up the learning curve. People will complain that their jobs are harder, or the old ways were better.

Not everything is going to work perfectly on the first try. This is adaptive learning. No one will know exactly what it will take to accomplish the goal, and no one will be able to anticipate all the changes required. Hitting stretch goals requires employing flexible methods while you maintain a steadfast focus on the goal.

Not every goal can be – or should be – a stretch goal. Because they're so radical, they're best used in a mix with more conventional, incremental goals. Striving for ten times improvement in every aspect of the organization diffuses focus and effort, creates change fatigue and can de-energize people rather than firing them up. Think about where "breaking the four-minute mile" will have the most impact – and set your stretch goal strategically where it will do the most good.

THOUGHT STARTER QUESTIONS

1. How aligned are your goals, or your team members' goals, to the strategy of your organization?
2. If you played 5-on-5, what would be the result? How many would match?
3. To what extent are each of your goals, and that of your team members, outlined in SET format?
4. What stretch goals do you have in your organization? What areas of your organization are most threatened by, or under attack from, disruptive competitors? What opportunities do you have to dramatically differentiate yourself from your competition? What stretch goals are required to do that?
5. Do the goals you and those of any of your direct reports contribute to the success of one or more of the major elements of the balanced scorecard?

FIRST STEPS

1. Play 5-on-5. (If you take NOTHING else from this book, you must do that!)

2. Look at the goals you and your direct reports have: To what extent are they "activity-based" goals versus Result-Oriented Goals. Figure out what the results of those activities should be; then make sure they align with the strategy of the organization.
3. Look at your goals, and/or those of your direct reports: Assess how well they fit the SET format:
   a. What is the Starting Point for each goal?
   b. What is the Ending Point for each goal?
   c. Does each of them have a Timeframe?
4. Identify the most critical stretch goal for your organization that either defends you from disruptive competition or allows you to capture a sustainable, defensible position in the marketplace. Energize the organization around that stretch goal (and, be ready for the disruption it will create).

BIBLIOGRAPHY

Coonradt, Charles A. & Nelson, Lee. (1984). *The Game of Work*. Park City, UT: Liberty Press.

Doran, G.T. There's a S.M.A.R.T Way to Write Management's Goals and Objectives. *Management Review (AMA Forum)* 70 (11): PP35–36.

Drucker, Peter. (May 1963) Managing for Business Effectiveness. *Harvard Business Review*, PP53–60.

Goldratt, Eliyahu M. & Cox, Jeff. (1984). *The Goal*. Great Barrington, MA: The North River Press.

John, F. Kennedy before a joint session of Congress, May 25, 1961.

Reichheld, Frederick F. (December 2003) The One Number You Need to Grow. *Harvard Business Review*.

Senge, Peter M. (1990). *The Fifth Discipline*. New York, NY: Doubleday/Currency.

6

Build Visible Scorecards: Improving Performance by Keeping Score

The old management maxim rings true, "What gets measured, gets done."

Imagine you're at a playground where two groups of kids are playing soccer on adjacent fields. On one field, the kids are keeping score. On another field, they aren't. How do you think the level of effort and performance will differ between the two fields? Even if you were far away, so you could only see, not hear, the action, how long would it take you to figure out which field was which? It probably wouldn't take long.

Keeping score naturally motivates people to play harder. It lets them know when their efforts are having an impact, and when they're falling short.

If we want to perform at our absolute best, we can't just go out and kick the ball around, we need to keep score. Keeping score in sports is easy. Keeping score in business – that's trickier. Sometimes it's hard to see a connection between our job details and the results. Still, there is a connection, and the things team members do each day deeply affect whether the company wins or loses.

That's why every individual and team in every organization needs a scorecard that makes this connection visible and clear to every team member.

Good scorecards drive performance. Perhaps more importantly, good scorecards foster learning. They allow performers and the organization to see the connection between performance and results, and then adjust performance to ensure it's delivering the critical results.

How do you design an effective scorecard? Start with a simple premise: People want to do work that matters. People perform better, and want to perform better, when they can see the connection between their efforts and the results they are achieving.

The Visible Scorecard Gear outlines how to ensure everyone has a scorecard that aligns to their critical Result-Oriented Goals, and is visible and available to the performers "during the game." This allows them to change the outcome of the game while it is still being played.

Visible Scorecards that ensure the right things get done share these characteristics:

1. (Good) Create a direct line of sight between performance and results.
2. (Better) Compare current performance, goals or standards, and all-time best performance.
3. (Best) Show trends over time.

GOOD SCORECARDS: CREATE A DIRECT LINE OF SIGHT BETWEEN PERFORMANCE AND RESULTS

The right scorecard creates a line of sight between the work people do and the execution of strategy. It helps make work matter and drive ownership and engagement at the same time.

We once visited a plant where a supervisor would review a computer printout of the team's production every day. Instead of sharing the results, he gave a fist pump when he was pleased with the results and a headshake when he wasn't. When we asked the team members what they learned from that, their response was unanimous: "Nothing." When we asked them how they had performed in terms of critical measures like overall output and quality, their uniform response was "We don't know."

In contrast, visit one of the dozens of Nucor steel mills across the United States. Walk into any pulpit during any shift, and team members can show you on multiple screens the production performance – nearly up to the minute – and the percent of production bonus earned by the crew for the week. This is one of the reasons that Nucor teammates are among the most productive in the steel industry: At any given moment, they can see the connection between their efforts and the results they generate for both Nucor and themselves.

People need to be able to see how their efforts directly impact results. It can't be filtered or made ambiguous. People take ownership when they can see the real data and can change the outcomes.

Quantitative Data is better than Qualitative Data...

In a football game, you don't need to judge the artistry of each team's passing attack to determine who's winning. You just look at the scoreboard. It doesn't always work this way in business. People get distracted by appearances and judge performance based on perception instead of results.

As an experiment, a friend of mine named Bill said he would do no work for two weeks yet still "earn" a reputation as the hardest-working person in the office.

For those two weeks, he arrived earlier and left later than everyone else. He shut his office door and spread paperwork, otherwise untouched, over his desk every day. He left his office only to refill his coffee, grab lunch out of the breakroom refrigerator, and hit the restroom. He walked fast. He avoided all small talk. "Gotta get back to work," was his ready made excuse.

The ploy worked. Soon you could hear the conversations around the water cooler:

"How's Bill performing?"

"Great!"

How do you know?"

"He looks like he's working hard."

Working hard but producing nothing. As the story illustrates, if we only measure performance based upon impressions instead of actual data, we can be misled.

Quantitative data makes it easier to compare actual performance with the goal, identify the most significant gaps that need attention, and measure their impact on the team or organization.

It's easier to keep score with quantitative measures of performance – units sold, product shipped, market share, units sold to key customers, variable costs, production yield, quality or on-time delivery.

THE FACTS MUST BE FRIENDLY

The purpose of a scorecard is to give team members the information they need to get better. For scorecards to be useful, team members must have nothing to fear from keeping accurate scorecard data, so long as they learn and improve.

Unfortunately, some organizations misuse their data. Since an effective scorecard identifies gaps between current performance and a team's goals, it's easy to look for someone to blame for the gap.

This creates an incentive for team members to fudge the data on their scorecards to make themselves look better, which defeats the entire purpose of a scorecard as a performance improvement tool. A scorecard can't tell you where you need to improve if the information is skewed to look better than it really is.

The facts must be friendly.

Our work with the resort we mentioned earlier is a great example of scorecards gone bad. The resort had 11 food and beverage outlets from concession stands to fine dining.

At the first monthly operating review with the outlet leaders, we noticed some intriguing data: The cost of food as a percentage of revenue in every one of the 11 operations was exactly the same: 37%.

There's no way this should have happened. Concession stand nachos should cost a lot less per sales dollar than the filet at the white tablecloth restaurant, even though the steak sells at a much higher price than the chip. Even if every outlet offered the exact same menu, variations in product sales should produce slightly different food-cost percentages for each outlet.

When we brought this up, the managers punted. No one said anything. They agreed that it was odd, and they would "do better next month." And they did. The next month, every one of the operations reported food costs at 36% of revenues, a 1 percentage point improvement across the board, with no variation once again among the outlets.

It was time to get to the bottom of this. After much conversation, we learned that the facts were NOT friendly. The restaurant leaders had all gotten in huge trouble any time they reported higher than expected food costs. There was no effort to learn what caused those numbers, only punishment for being out of line.

So, the group figured out how to avoid the tongue lashings. When every manager reported the same food costs, nobody got in trouble. To make sure they had the same food costs, they moved inventory around at the end of the month until their food costs were identical. This typically took them until about 3 a.m.

This story actually reflected well on the managers in many ways. They cared a lot for each other and worked hard to protect one another. They had excellent business acumen. They knew exactly what moves to make to get the numbers to all balance out. They had a great work ethic, scrambling until 3 a.m. to pull off their magic trick of uniform food costs across the resort. Yet, their efforts made it impossible to understand how the restaurants were truly performing.

The key lesson is this: If facts aren't friendly, if they are used to threaten instead of guide, people will alter the measurement process and render the data useless.

For your scorecards to be effective, remember data rules and keep the facts friendly.

...but Qualitative Data Can Work

Sometimes you do need to rely on qualitative data, such as how much restaurant patrons like the food, or the value a client feels an accountant or other professional service provider adds to his company, or how well team members feel their leaders engage them. In cases like these, perception is reality.

We can use tools such as surveys to translate people's qualitative perceptions into quantitative data. At best, these will yield a rough approximation – directionally correct – of their true feelings. But over time, multiple measurements can provide useful information. Customers feel the clothing we're selling is not as stylish as it was a year ago, or our clients are more excited about our ad campaigns than they've been the previous two years. Converting qualitative data into quantitative data, even a crude approximation of quantitative data, can point the way to improvement.

Note that there is a huge difference between "qualitative" data and your personal opinion. Effective qualitative data is gathered from the perspective of the people best prepared to provide accurate information. It's not from your perspective just based on how you feel you're doing or how you feel someone on your team is doing.

A few examples:

Early in my career, I led an engineering team at Pacific Gas and Electric. Our team was responsible for the engineering and construction of new gas and/or services to customers. We had a crappy reputation over the length of time it took to get new services installed. Our average was about 12 weeks. We went all out to drive that number down.

It took about six months, but we finally reduced the time to just eight weeks. We're slapping high fives celebrating our great success. Then, we talked to our customers. Many of them were still upset. While cycle times had improved for many of them, others were still upset because even eight weeks was too long to wait for the farmer who needed power to a well to keep his crops growing. Others could easily wait longer. We had made the mistake of focusing on the average, and what we thought was important, instead of the unique needs of individual customers.

Later, as a consultant, I worked with a client on a marketing project. The leaders wanted to understand the factors that caused customers to choose their company over its key competitors. They conducted extensive interviews with both internal team members and their customers. When they looked at the top five choice factors for each group, they found no overlap between what customers thought was most important and what the internal team members thought was most important.

Another client we worked with thought it was the best in its industry for on-time delivery. The company's team members would often describe it as a competitive advantage. When they asked their customers, they found they were among the worst.

Qualitative or Quantitative, the Data Must be Visible and Timely

The data must be visible, so performers can see when and how to adjust to produce the desired results.

It doesn't do much good if we keep the score a secret from the players, and it doesn't do much good if players don't see the score until after the game is over – as in, being told on May 3 that you missed your April sales goal by 15%. Imagine a bowler trying to pick up the spare when she can't see which pins are still standing.

When we first started working with the resort, it was bleeding cash and customers. One of the key obstacles to a rebound was the timeliness of the data leadership was using. Managers were receiving labor cost data ten days after the end of each month – way too late for them to respond. They knew the resort was overspending on labor by roughly $200,000 each month – cash they absolutely couldn't afford to waste. In each monthly business review, they would address the issue with their leadership team. Every month the leaders would promise "to do a better job" managing labor costs. But, really, they couldn't. They didn't have the tools to match revenue to labor to change the game while it was still being played.

They asked their Information Technology (IT) group to create a way to see the connection between revenue and labor cost daily for every one of their 50 operations. The IT group said they could do that, but it would take one year and cost more than $1 million. The resort had neither the time nor the money to afford that solution, so they went old school. They asked each of the 50 leaders to track labor hours for their units each day and report by 8 a.m. the next morning their labor hours from the day before. Using that data, based on average labor rates, they were able to respond with fresh reports by noon comparing the day's actual labor costs versus what they should have been based upon guest traffic and volume.

Once they began receiving these daily reports, how long do you think it took for labor costs to fall in line? One day! Literally less than 24 hours. The 50 leaders received the first summary report at noon on the first day. That afternoon they began changing their staffing to better match the volume of business. That's the power of providing people with the right data to gauge performance, and change the game while it's still being played.

Changing What You're Scoring

How frequently does a scorecard need to be updated? That depends on the value of the information, the cost of acquiring it, and the speed with which performance can change.

In the case of the resort, monthly updates were too infrequent, but hourly updates would have been unnecessary. Many manufacturers, though, might require minute-by-minute performance updates to instantly address quality or productivity issues before they produce too many poor-quality items.

For a broad metric like market share, monthly or even quarterly data might be optimal, since measuring results more frequently likely would be expensive and unreliable.

To make your scorecard visible and available while the game is being played, think about how frequently people need the information so that they can adjust their performance on a timely basis. Think about where the data must come from. Finally, think about how you make that information available to the performers.

BETTER SCORECARDS: COMPARE CURRENT PERFORMANCE, THE GOALS OR STANDARDS, AND THE ALL-TIME BEST PERFORMANCE

Scorecards that provide comparisons create perspective. They don't simply report data. They compare data with something – a goal, an employee's best-ever performance or some other benchmark.

Let's revisit the production manager who fist-pumped and shook his head to communicate results. Now let's say he upgraded to, "Our production quality today was 75% good with no defects."

Well, that is definitely quantitative. It's better than a fist pump. But his answer is not as helpful as it could be. We might also want to know:

- How does 75% compare to what customers expect from their products?
- How does today's quality compare to the best the company has ever done?
- How does 75% compare with a month ago, three months ago, or a year ago? Is the number rising, falling, or staying about the same? More on this item will be discussed later in the chapter.

Knowing the answers to those questions would help the company understand the true impact of the day's performance.

Let's say a nationwide paper manufacturer has a market share in the Northeast of 20%. It's good to know that. But what if it's 25% in other markets? What if the company's best-ever Northeastern market share was 30%?

Knowing those numbers will help us ask the right questions, such as:

- Why is our share lower in the Northeast?
- What actions do we need to take to get it to 25% or even higher?
- What happened that caused our share to drop from the 30% we used to have?
- What, if anything, should we do to get that lost share back?

To be truly effective, your scorecard needs to go beyond merely providing a point-in-time view of performance. Numbers telling you how many units you produced today, or how many units you sold this week are good to know.

But without comparisons they don't provide insights into the difference, if any, between where performance is and where it ought to be.

When you first build your scorecard, you will sometimes find that you don't know what the acceptable standard, or goal, should be. That's okay. You may also not know what your best-ever performance was. That's okay, too. (For that matter, as we help clients build Visible Scorecards that reflect their strategies, we often find they don't even know what current performance is for some items.) But you will want to put some effort into figuring out what the goal ought to be. To establish the "best-ever" performance, you can either look back or, if that's not practical, just let the information accumulate over time as you establish newer, and higher, levels of performance.

For operational and financial scorecard items, you might look at your competitors or another company in a similar industry for guidance. What are their conversion costs, yields, productivity, and safety numbers? What is the best you've ever done on these measures? Together, this information should lead you to a reasonable goal for your business or team.

Or perhaps the answer lies with your customers. What do they consider acceptable or outstanding quality or on-time delivery performance? Who's the best on various customer choice factors? How do you compare to them?

A great example of how to effectively use comparisons in scorecards comes from former NBA coach Pat Riley. Riley had an incredibly successful career in the NBA as a player and a coach who led the Los Angeles

Lakers through four championship seasons, then took the New York Knicks and later the Miami Heat to the NBA Finals and one more title.

In his book, *The Winner Within*,[1] the Hall-of-Famer talks about the "Career Best Efforts" scorecards that were developed for each member of the Los Angeles Lakers during their 1980s championships years.

First, each scorecard was specific to the individual player, his role, and his goals.

Second, the scorecards were available while the game was being played. Each player was given an up-to-date version of his scorecard at halftime and then again immediately after every game.

Third, each scorecard contained information about the player's current game performance, his target performance, and his career best-ever performance.

This helped ensure that every team member knew how he was contributing to the team's performance and helped keep him motivated to hit his goals and continue to push up his best performance.

Returning to the production manager, now he might respond to, "How was the production quality today?" with:

"It was 75%. We were below target because our customers have said we need to consistently hit 85% – which is our acceptable standard – for them to be fully comfortable placing orders with us. It's also below our best-ever quality performance of 87%."

The production manager and anyone posing the question both know that work must still be done to improve the team's quality to a consistently acceptable level. Adding an acceptable standard and best-ever performance to your scorecard will help you and your team achieve your best.

BEST SCORECARDS: SHOW TRENDS OVER TIME

So far, we've discussed building scorecards that are:

- As quantitative as possible.
- Visible.

---

[1] *The Winner Within*, Pat Riley, G.P. Putnam's Sons, New York, NY, 1993.

- Available for use while the game is being played.
- Able to compare current performance to an accepted standard, goal or target, and best-ever performance.

Scorecards that fit those criteria are very good and will be very helpful for driving execution.

The best scorecards also show trends in performance over time, which makes the information in the scorecard even more meaningful.

Trends allow you to see:

- Whether performance is improving or declining.
- How different scorecard items are moving relative to each other.

Let's go back to our production manager one final time. We know that his team's most recent performance was 75% good quality, that its goal is 85% and its best-ever performance was 87%. That tells us a lot more than we knew before, but it still doesn't tell us everything. We can't see whether the team is getting better, getting worse, or staying about the same.

Looking at the team's performance over time would allow us to see any patterns in its quality performance, which might provide some hints about how to improve it.

Let's say the production manager reviews two different scenarios of a report showing production quality levels over the last four weeks.

In Scenario A, he would see that production quality is generally getting better, that many days are at or above the acceptable standard and that today's 75% quality result was a significant step below the team's typical performance. He could then look into what happened today that caused that problem (Figure 6.1).

In Scenario B, the story is very different. Quality performance has trended down over the last few weeks, indicating that something significant has likely changed in the work process (Figure 6.2).

So, as the production manager expands his scorecard to look at trends over time, he learns much more. This helps find the root cause of his team's quality issues.

To assemble trend data, consider the timeframe in which trends would be most meaningful, just as we did when we considered the frequency of data capture for the scorecard.

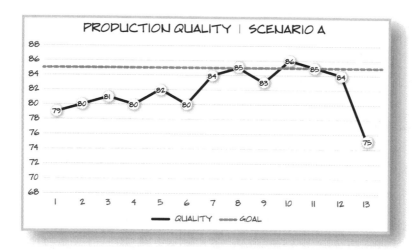

FIGURE 6.1
Production Quality: Scenario A

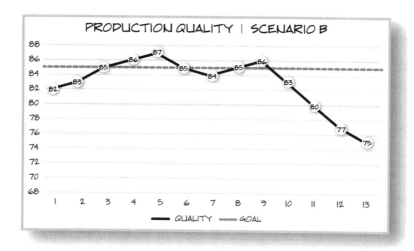

FIGURE 6.2
Production Quality: Scenario B

Looking at trends also allows you to look for correlations to other sets of data. Let's return to the example of the paper manufacturer that wants to grow market share in the Northeast back to its best-ever level of 30%. Correlating market share to a critical financial metric like gross margin is important. As can be seen in the following two charts, the company's market share has grown, but gross margins have decreased over the same time period (Figures 6.3 and 6.4).

Being armed with that information allows the organization to learn:

- Whether the company was merely buying market share with lower pricing and, therefore, actually hurting profits, or
- If something else was driving the decreases in gross margin (e.g., higher variable costs).

To recap what we learned about building your scorecard, remember to create scorecards that:

- Provide a direct line of site between performance and results.
- Are available and visible while the game is being played so you can alter your performance to achieve better results.
- Use quantitative data whenever possible.

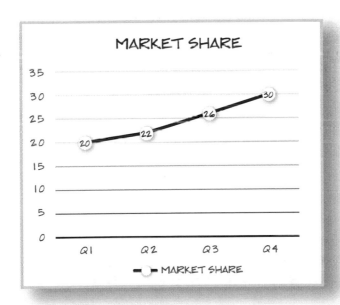

FIGURE 6.3
Market Share Up...

FIGURE 6.4
...But Gross Margins Decline

- Use qualitative data where that makes the most sense.
- Are used to guide learning and improvement, not punish.
- Provide comparisons between current performance and an acceptable standard (like a goal or target) and your best-ever performance.
- Show trend data, not just point-in-time information, whenever possible.

THOUGHT STARTER QUESTIONS

1. What actions do you take, or what do you pay attention to, that may create misunderstandings about the key priorities within your organization?

2. How visible are the scorecards within your organization? Do people get the information they need to alter the outcome of the game while it's still being played?

3. To what extent do the scorecards within your organization provide clear information about:
   a. Current performance.
   b. The goal, target, or an acceptable standard.
   c. Best-ever performance.

4. To what extent do the scorecards in your organization show trends to enable you to spot patterns and correlations over time?

5. To what extent do people in your organization "own" their scorecards and feel responsible for improving results relative to them?

6. What unintended consequences, if any, occur as a result of the scorecards you have in place?

7. Are there items you would like to measure to support your organization's strategy that you can't or don't measure today? What do you need to do to get those metrics in place?

FIRST STEPS

1. Identify all the scorecards that people are using on a daily or weekly basis.
   a. Do they give people the information they need on a timely basis to make the most effective decisions?
   b. To what extent are the scorecards aligned with your individual, team, department, or organization's goals and strategy?
   c. What goals or other items that are critical to your strategy are not currently reflected in your scorecards?

2. Identify the 1–3 critical metrics for each of your goals.

3. Build a tracking system to make sure you have the data you need for each of those metrics to make decisions and take action on a timely basis.

4. For each goal and metric, identify:
   a. Current performance.
   b. The goal, target, or acceptable standard.

    c. Your best-ever performance (or the best performance by a bench-mark organization).

5. Build a dashboard of your metrics showing the trends in the critical metrics side by side. Regularly look for trends and correlations between the scorecard items.

BIBLIOGRAPHY

Coonradt, Charles A. & Benson, Lee. (1998). *Scorekeeping for Success.* Park City, UT: The Game of Work, Inc.

Riley, Pat. (1993). *The Winner Within.* New York, NY: G. P. Putnam's Sons.

Waterman, Jr., Robert H. (1987). *The Renewal Factor.* New York, NY: Bantam Books, Inc.

7

Define the Performance Drivers: The Critical Activities That Lead to the Right Results

Once there was a town that had only two pizza parlors. Mario owned one and his brother, Tony, the other. Both used their mother's recipe. Both used fresh ingredients from local suppliers. In general, people loved their pizza. And, really, there wasn't much difference between the two parlors.

To one-up his brother, Tony made it his goal to have the fastest delivery in town. Tony drilled his employees until they could take an order in seconds and prepare a pizza in minutes, and he hired the fastest, safest drivers in town. He kept scorecards on a bulletin board and rewarded the shift managers with the best on-time delivery record. Tony's averaged delivering a pizza in 40 minutes – half the time it took Mario on a busy night.

Soon, Tony's was getting the lion's share of the town's pizza orders, and he ultimately bought his brother's place.

Tony's monopoly did not last long. The next year, Perfecto Pizza opened a location nearby, and Tony saw his orders drop. Perfecto focused on a market positioning strategy of decent pizza, cheap. It used canned and packaged products from a food distribution company. Because it used canned, pre-packaged ingredients, Perfecto could make and deliver a pizza in 30 minutes and charge less.

Tony thought he had to beat Perfecto on delivery time. So, he obsessively fine-tuned his process and held his employees to even faster standards until they could sometimes deliver a pizza in just 20 minutes.

It didn't help. Tony lost even more business to Perfecto. One day, Tony asked his friend: "What can I do? We can't deliver any faster than this."

His friend sighed and said, "I don't know how to tell you this, Tony, but everybody I talk to is frustrated doing business with you. The variability in your product drives your customers nuts. In the past, your pizzas were exquisitely made. But now, because you're often in a hurry, everybody has a story about receiving pizzas with the wrong toppings or a sparse amount of sausage or cheese. Frankly, people are happy to wait an extra 10 minutes to get a consistent, predictable pizza a little cheaper from Perfecto."

It might seem like Tony did everything right. He had a good strategy that differentiated him first from Mario and then later from Perfecto. He set Result-Oriented Goals, posted scorecards so his staff could track and improve their delivery speed, and rewarded managers based on their team's delivery performance.

But in focusing solely on delivery speed, Tony neglected other factors that affected the consistency of his product.

In short, Tony failed because the Performance Drivers – what people actually DO – were not aligned with his strategy. He had the best pizza. When he focused his team's Performance Drivers on making great pizza, he had a competitive advantage. When all his focus went to Delivery Speed, he lost to Perfecto.

Driving Strategy to Execution to Results comes down to what people DO. Performance Drivers define what people do at every level of the organization to best execute the organization's strategy and deliver the right RESULTS.

At the organization level, Performance Drivers might be strategic initiatives designed to carve out that organization's competitive position in the marketplace, such as:

- Specific projects to improve performance.
- Actions by individual leaders that focus on critical outcomes and direct attention toward understanding the barriers people face in executing.
- Department or team initiatives for improving sales or service delivery, driving down costs, improving quality performance, and supporting schedule fidelity.

Performance Drivers are, in short, those few critical behaviors or actions that distinguish between average and great performance.

Michael Porter said that strategy "means deliberately choosing a different set of activities to deliver a unique mix of value." The concept of Performance Drivers cascades the idea of "choosing a different set of activities" to every level of the organization.

The Performance Driver Gear logically follows the previous two Performance Gears: Result-Oriented Goals and Visible Scorecard. You identify Performance Drivers that allow you to most effectively and efficiently move the needles on the scorecard and hit the goals.

People love to DO stuff. For many people, the tangible act of doing stuff is way easier than thinking about their goals and then identifying the critical behaviors (aka, Performance Drivers) that give them the greatest opportunity to hit those goals. However, without putting energy and focus into identifying the right Performance Drivers, team members' behavior is often diffused and unfocused.

Focusing on the Performance Drivers is a concept that is essentially embodied in "The Process" made famous by Nick Saban, coach of the Alabama Crimson Tide, a perennial championship favorite in college football. As Saban described it to Ryan Holiday, author of the book *The Obstacle is the Way*,[1] "Don't think about winning the SEC Championship. Don't think about the national championship. Think about what you needed to do in this drill, on this play, at this moment. That's the process: Let's think about what we can do today, the task at hand."

Contrast that with many organizations in which people often seem like pinballs reacting to one stimulus or crisis before being hit by another. Effective execution becomes impossible. As a senior executive in a Fortune 500-sized company once told me, "We're great at taking the hill. The problem is we often don't think about what hill we're taking or why we're taking it."

Once the Performance Drivers have been identified, leaders can then focus on helping team members execute them effectively and consistently by building their capabilities through training, development, and Purposeful/Deliberate practice.

There are four critical components to identifying and executing the Performance Drivers that apply at every level of the organization:

---

[1] *The Obstacle Is the Way*, Ryan Holiday, Penguin Group, New York, NY, 2014.

- Determine the Performance Drivers.
- Master execution of the Performance Drivers: Purposeful and Deliberate Practice.
- Track execution of the Performance Drivers.
- Regularly reassess your Performance Drivers.

Let's look at each one of those in turn.

DETERMINE THE PERFORMANCE DRIVERS

So, how do you figure out the Performance Drivers for your organization? We'll focus on three common approaches.

Identify the Behaviors that Separate Great from Average Performers

In a food and beverage operation we worked with, the restaurant was receiving customer complaints about tables set with dirty glasses, silverware, or plates. Managers responded by setting a goal for the kitchen stewards – the people responsible for washing dishes – to "put 100% clean dishes on the table." They developed a 27-step process for getting clean dishes to the table every time.

The process didn't have the impact they hoped for. So, they reassessed. They identified the steward who was doing the best job of getting clean plates to the table; he was only following 8 of the 27 steps.

Looking even deeper, they found that one step, inspecting the plates after they came out of the dishwasher, was more important that all the others combined. The other steps were important for ensuring that the dishes were sanitary and ready for use, but that one step – inspection – was most critical to ensuring that only clean plates made it to the table. Armed with a simpler process – but one with a strong correlation to meeting the goal – the restaurant fixed the issue.

This is also a great example of how Result-Oriented Goals allow team members to take ownership of the processes and results. In this case, it was a frontline team member who identified the critical step in the process and changed it to improve quality and drive out unnecessary steps.

What do great performers do differently that sets them apart?

On many work teams, you often will find one or two people who deliver significantly better results than others. They're the ones everyone else counts on when work gets difficult or deadlines loom. A great performer can be an individual, or it can be an entire division or business unit.

Sometimes these "expert performers" might possess some rare talent, but usually they have the same capabilities as their teammates. They're just approaching the work in a different way.

In golf, it's easy to tell a great performer from a hacker – just compare where the ball goes. I'm clearly closer to hacker territory than pro. However, by identifying the right Performance Drivers, and instituting the principles of Deliberate Practice, I was able to cut my handicap in half in a relatively short period of time. (See the sidebar "From Hacker to Mediocre Golfer in Less than Six Months," later in this chapter.)

What is true for golf, is true for many other activities. Whether it's selling, invoice processing, manufacturing, preparing a presentation, or keeping a client happy, there are things that great performers do that produce better results.

If we recognize the great performers, identify the critical behaviors that they do differently and teach them to the rest of the team, the entire organization can raise its game.

By asking what great performance looks like and studying great performers, we can open our minds, see the same tasks in a new light, and find new ways to achieve our goals. It's critical not to let your ego get in the way of learning. We've seen dozens of people perform far below their potential by thinking, "Yeah, we may have problems, but I've got my shit together. It's all those other people that need to change." Making the changes necessary to master your Performance Drivers can be difficult and humbling. You often have to be willing to be uncomfortable and feel clumsy to yield dramatic improvement.

Look Outside (Your Organization)

What if you don't have anyone in your organization that really stands out? What if it's not obvious what your standouts do differently, or it's difficult for the rest of the team to adopt their techniques? You might have to look beyond your organization and instead identify a leader in your industry. If you're a small business owner, what are the industry leaders doing differently from you? The reverse works, too: if you're an industry leader, what are the upstarts in your industry doing differently?

You might even look outside your industry. If you believe customer service, for example, could be a Performance Driver, perhaps you can find a customer service role model in another business altogether and adapt that organization's techniques. Have you stayed in a nice hotel lately? How do they approach customer service? Whether you're talking about coding software, taking care of customers, or building a quality product, what are the best-in-class doing differently from you?

Think about Table 7.1 and how it might apply to your organization. Who's the Best in Show for those items? What is it about their practices that could shape your Performance Drivers?

Blow It Up

Sometimes when you're stuck, the best thing to do is shake things up.

We once worked with a theme park that wanted to dramatically improve the guest experience, so it could compete more effectively against a competitor who had a famous mouse as a mascot.

As part of the project, we pulled together leaders representing a cross-section of the organization. We asked them to identify all the things they thought the organization ought to STOP doing: All the rules, policies, and procedures that get in the way of delivering better guest experiences.

The group identified 220 items within a couple hours. We asked the company president to join us for the debriefing. He sat in the back of the room as people went through their lists. At the end, we asked him for his

TABLE 7.1

What Is It about Their Practices that Could Shape Your Performance Drivers?

	(A) Our Industry	(B) Any Industry
1. Producing our services or goods		
2. Driving down operating costs		
3. Marketing and sales		
4. Quality management processes and performance		
5. On-time delivery		
6. Safety		
7. Customer service		

reaction. He admitted, "It was painful. First, understand that I agree that most of those 220 items make no sense. They absolutely get in the way of better guest experiences. But here's why they cause me so much pain. I've been here as long as this park has been here. I started as a parking lot attendant and worked my way up. I've worked at every level of this organization and in every department. I either wrote, reviewed or authorized almost every one of those 220 items. And, each one made absolute sense at the time. But, sitting here listening to you outline the list, I'm thinking, 'That's the dumbest thing we've ever done. What was I thinking?' So, yeah, this is pretty painful."

The organization went on to eliminate most of the items on the list. The ones they didn't eliminate they tried to modify to improve the guest experience. And they clearly explained the rationale behind the ones that remained so that everyone understood the why behind the what.

You might be thinking, "If it's not broke, don't fix it." As that situation clearly illustrated, a lot of times "it" needs breaking.

In another situation, we were engaged by the HR department of an organization to assess, from their stakeholders' perspective, the value of all the work they did. What we found was that only about 40% of what the group did create value for any of their stakeholders, even senior leadership. They were spending 60% of their time on tasks that weren't Performance Drivers.

To blow it up, start with this question: "If we weren't tied to the way we do things today, and we could start all over, what would be the most effective and efficient way to accomplish our goals?"

Involve new team members in the conversation, or even people from outside the work group – people who might not be as tied to the old ways. These people often can bring new perspectives that challenge the status quo.

MASTER EXECUTION OF THE PERFORMANCE DRIVERS: PURPOSEFUL AND DELIBERATE PRACTICE

It's not enough merely to know what your Performance Drivers are. The individuals and organizations that are the best at translating execution to results are constantly honing the skills and capabilities necessary to execute those Performance Drivers to perfection. It's one thing for Michael Jordan to know that hitting a fade-away jump shot from the low post area would enable him to be one of the greatest, if not the greatest, basketball players of all time. The countless hours of deliberately practicing that jump shot is what made him that good.

Going back to Chapter 2: Right, Right, Right, it's also one reason organizations that want to consistently drive Strategy to Execution to Results must commit to constantly upgrading the talents and capabilities of their team members. The skills required for success today are not the skills that will be required for success in the future. To attract and retain talent, and to put people in the best position to be successful, organizations must commit to constant growth and improvement in their skills and capabilities.

In *Peak: Secrets from the New Science of Expertise*,[2] author K. Anders Ericsson says, "In pretty much any area of human endeavor, people have a tremendous capacity to improve their performance, as long as they train the right way…. How much you improve is up to you." (This might sound familiar to many readers. Malcom Gladwell attempted to capture the essence of Ericsson's research in the now famous "10,000-hour rule" that he outlined in his book *Outliers*.)

So, what does that have to do with Performance Drivers? Performance Drivers are the critical tasks, behaviors, and actions people take to perform their best. But most people don't necessarily master the skills and capabilities to perform their best. Many of us engage in what Ericsson describes as "naïve practice" … just doing the same things over and over with no focus on improvement.

It may not be "mastery" in the sense of being a chess grand master or being able to play violin with the New York Philharmonic orchestra, but by identifying the right Performance Drivers and then deliberately practicing the right stuff, most people can get a lot better, lifting their organizations with them.

- Salespeople can sell better.
- Customer service reps can deliver better customer service.
- Programmers can code better.
- Leaders can better engage their teams and deliver better results.

---

[2] *Peak: Secrets from the New Science of Expertise*, Andres Ericsson and Robert Pool, Houghton Mifflin Harcourt, New York, NY, 2017.

Ericsson describes the potential this way:

> Imagine what might be possible if we applied the techniques that have proved to be so effective in sports and music and chess to all the different types of learning that people do, from the education of school children to the training of doctors, engineers, pilots, business people and workers of every sort. I believe that dramatic improvements we have seen in those few fields over the past hundred years are achievable in pretty much every field if we apply the lessons that can be learned from studying the principles of effective practice.

Ericsson describes two levels of practice that can move performance far beyond the limits of naïve practice. The first is Purposeful Practice, in which:

- Performers set well-defined, specific goals (think SET Result-Oriented Goals from Chapter 5).
- Performance Drivers break down into the micro skills/behaviors required for success. Then, you practice improving each of those skills in concentrated ways.
- Everyone gives and receives feedback including the performer.
- Everyone gets used to being uncomfortable.

Deliberate Practice then adds two more elements:

- The field is well-established with critical skills that have been identified over a significant period (years, decades, or even centuries).
- There are experts who serve as teachers and coaches who have developed training techniques that enable ever-increasing skill levels.

FROM HACKER TO MEDIOCRE GOLFER IN LESS THAN SIX MONTHS: MY EXPERIENCE WITH DELIBERATE PRACTICE

Like many people, I took up golf after college. I was not good. Over the first few (okay, 20) years, I got a little better, but not much.

I finally got tired of playing poorly, so I made a commitment to getting better. My first action was to SET a Result-Oriented Goal to *reduce my handicap from 30 to 15 within 6 months.*

Then, it got down to the Performance Drivers – what I needed to DO differently to improve.

To help with that, I hired a golf pro who helped me develop a much better, more consistent swing. Golf is a game for which the critical skills have been developed over decades. Many golf pros have developed training techniques to transfer those skills to others.

This is where getting comfortable with being uncomfortable came in. In our first session, the pro changed everything about my swing: grip, stance, posture, takeaway, etc. In that lesson, I went from comfortable ... and not being able to hit worth a damn ... to being really, really uncomfortable, yet able to hit pretty well and much more consistently. I was so uncomfortable, both mentally and physically, that I felt like I would fall over just standing over the ball.

But for the first time in my life, I could hit balls in the right direction, with the right shape and better distance, much more consistently.

Finally, the feedback portion: Initially, the feedback about what I was doing well and not well came from the pro. As I began to understand my swing better, I was able to give feedback to myself and then make the appropriate adjustments.

Without knowing what it was called, the pro and I applied all the components of Deliberate Practice.

The result: My handicap did fall from 30 to 15, and in well less than 6 months. Was I going to become a professional level golfer? No chance. But I was able to improve my performance dramatically by following the principles of Deliberate Practice.

(See the sidebar, "From Hacker to Mediocre Golfer in Less than Six Months," for my real-life experience with Deliberate Practice.)

Sales training represents one of the more prevalent applications of Deliberate Practice in organizations. There must be thousands of sales training programs. Many of them apply the principles of Deliberate Practice (Table 7.2).

There are similar opportunities to build skills and capabilities through Purposeful or Deliberate Practice whether it's coding software, practicing medicine, operating a production line in a manufacturing facility, or delivering exceptional customer service.

TABLE 7.2

Typical Sales Training as Deliberate Practice

Goals	Many require participants to set specific improvement goals.
Micro skills/behaviors	Almost all outline a selling process with specific behaviors along the process: effective prospecting, asking high-impact questions, creating a high-impact sales presentation, negotiating and closing the sale. The participants practice under the watchful eye of a sales trainer or coach.
Feedback	Most programs are feedback-intensive. Participants often provide their own feedback and then get more feedback from other participants and from trainers/coaches.
Being uncomfortable	There is usually much discomfort as participants practice new skills or take existing skills to higher levels.
Well-established critical skills	While programs will differ in terms of some aspects of the skills they teach – that's sales training programs trying to create their own competitive advantage (!) – most of them share a common core set of skills that have developed over many years.
Experts as teachers and coaches	Many of the programs are led by teachers or sales coaches who have refined their techniques over long periods of time.

Identifying the Performance Drivers and following the process of Purposeful or Deliberate Practice can help boost the results anyone delivers in any field. Use:

Purposeful Practice – when you can break your Performance Drivers down into smaller sets of behaviors and skills that enable higher levels of performance. Then, engage others in helping you improve and providing the feedback necessary for success.

Deliberate Practice – when the Performance Driver requires skills that have been identified and developed over significant periods of time AND you can identify a teacher or coach (inside or outside your organization) who has developed training techniques that can help you grow your capabilities.

TRACK EXECUTION OF THE PERFORMANCE DRIVERS

Once you define your Performance Drivers, the next step is to track how well you are executing them.

Tracking Performance Drivers is critical to achieving results for three reasons. Tracking:

- Builds discipline for execution.
- Validates the connection between behavior and results.
- Spotlights early warning signs of a performance drop and helps diagnose the problem.

Most of us are horrible at tracking the execution of our Performance Drivers. So, let's talk about how tracking helps build discipline for execution.

Suppose that someone sets a goal to lose 10 pounds in the next two months. Given that it has a clear start point, a clear end point, and a timeframe, that's a pretty well-defined Results-Oriented Goal.

There are two universally recognized, effective Performance Drivers of losing weight: controlling what you eat and exercising.

So, if we know what we want to do and how to do it, why do so many people struggle to lose those excess pounds? In many cases, it's because they don't track their behaviors. They may feel like they are managing what they eat, but actually there is a big gap between how much they think they are eating and how much they really eat (Figure 7.1).

Once they begin tracking, people's behavior often improves, and they will make steadier progress toward their goal. The mere act of tracking helps instill the discipline necessary to execute consistently on the Performance Drivers.

In a typical workplace, most of us are surrounded by dozens of people and tasks competing for our attention. Many of us face a barrage of emails and text messages. Some of us – you know who you are – are constantly checking social media posts; reports need to be prepared; coworkers ask for help (some of which may not be directly related to either your or their Performance Drivers); and emergencies or requests from managers need to be handled.

We go home exhausted from all the activity, yet we spent precious little time on our Performance Drivers.

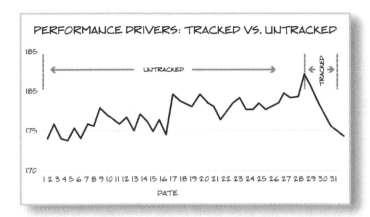

FIGURE 7.1
Results when tracking versus not tracking critical Performance Drivers.

We worked with one leader who said she felt like a pinball bounced from bumper to bumper all day, overwhelmingly busy. But, she said, "At the end of the day, I can't tell you one thing I've actually accomplished."

We often challenge leaders to track their actual time for a few days and compare it to their Performance Drivers. This forces them to look at the gap between what they are doing and what they should be doing to deliver the critical results for their organization. In one heart-wrenching situation, we worked with a leader whose marriage was on the rocks and his relationship with his kids was non-existent. He was the leader of a several-hundred-person organization. He typically got to the office by 6:30 a.m. and left for home around 6 p.m. He would have dinner with his family and then work remotely until 10 or so. No wonder his personal relationships were suffering.

When we asked him to chart his time and compare it to his personal leadership Performance Drivers, one factor stood out: He was spending far more time doing the work of his direct reports than he was leading them. His day was consumed with responding to emails to provide direction, holding conference calls where he was providing direction, or leading meetings with his team in which he was (you guessed it) providing direction.

Armed with that shocking, tangible gap, he was able to quickly change how he spent his time. He stopped pouncing on every email and focused on leading his team. He pushed responsibility back to his team in meetings or web conferences. He learned to step in only when appropriate, which became less necessary over time. As a result, his team performed better, and he was able to dramatically reduce the amount of time working both at the office and at home. Almost magically, his relationship with his wife and children improved.

Tracking provides an early warning system for declining performance. Think of a football coach breaking down game film. The coach might spot an offensive lineman's sloppy footwork and correct it before it turns into quarterback sacks on Sunday.

There is usually a strong correlation between players consistently executing their assigned tasks with the proper technique – every time – and how the team performs throughout the game. Put another way, consistent and effective execution of key Performance Drivers generally leads to a better result.

Now, most organizations don't have the benefit of reviewing films of their team members' performance. But we can approximate that type of analysis by asking three questions every day: What are our goals? What are the results? And what did we DO to accomplish those goals?

Keep It Simple

When tracking Performance Drivers, the most important thing is to keep it simple. If the time and energy required to track the Performance Drivers ends up distracting us from executing on those Performance Drivers, that defeats their purpose. Ideally, we can make the process simple enough to get the information we need without affecting our performance.

For the person trying to lose 10 pounds, spending two minutes per meal or workout tracking her calories and exercise on a mobile app is worth the effort if it helps her stick to her plan. For a salesperson, spending five minutes after every sales call to record key notes and follow-up items to increase the chance of a sale is worth the effort. But if the salesperson needs a half-hour to log each call, that's a lot of time taken away from the next sales call. The "cost" of tracking may be greater than the value of the information.

As with scorecards, you need to make your tracking system readily available and visible. That makes it easier to stay disciplined about tracking on a regular basis. It also makes it easier to see how you are doing and decide if you need to step up your effort or change your approach.

Finally, you want to step back and look at the correlation between your Performance Drivers and results. For a sales rep, it could mean looking at the connection between building account plans and preparing for each sales call and their monthly or quarterly sales results. If the correlation isn't strong, that's an indicator that whatever you're measuring might not be a Performance Driver and is not producing the necessary results.

And that leads to...

REGULARLY REASSESS YOUR PERFORMANCE DRIVERS

Performance Drivers typically need to change for one of three reasons:

- The execution of your Performance Drivers is not, or is no longer, leading to the results you want to achieve.
- You achieve your goals and want to take performance to a higher level.
- Your goals have changed due to a change in performance requirements or expanding expectations.

Execution of the Performance Drivers Isn't Delivering the Right Results

Let's look at the first case – where the execution of your Performance Drivers is not leading to the results you want to achieve. That's an excellent indication that you either:

- Haven't found the right Performance Drivers or
- You're not executing them consistently enough.

If you're tracking your Performance Drivers, you should be able to tell which of the two is correct.

I first learned this lesson playing middle school basketball. Like many of my teammates, I was a pretty mediocre foul shooter, averaging around 65% made. Our coach wanted us to improve, and he started our improvement effort with a bad, activity-based (the horror!) goal: "Shoot 100 free throws at the end of every practice." We were a group of young teenage boys, starving at the end of a two-hour basketball practice. This drill quickly devolved into chaos. Our objective was to get out of the gym and get home to food as quickly as possible. We shot some ugly, but very fast, free throws.

It didn't take long for the coach to see the error in his ways. First, he changed the goal. It went from "Shoot 100 free throws" (an activity) to "Make 100 free throws before you leave practice" (a Result-Oriented Goal with an imprecise but effective timeframe). Then, he asked us to track the execution of our Performance Drivers by requiring us to track the number of shots we had to take to make 100. (Our tracking system was to use a pencil to record the number of shots daily on the cinder block wall behind the basket.) Within a practice or two, our results began to improve. With a Result-Oriented Goal, an understanding of the key Performance Drivers and a tracking system, our coach devoted his attention to Deliberate Practice – helping us develop the skills to improve. In a few weeks, our team free-throw percentage moved from the 60% range to about 75%.

You've Achieved Your Goal and Want to Take Performance to a Higher Level

As a Nordstrom store general manager once said, "Good enough is not good enough."

With customer/stakeholder expectations constantly changing, performance expectations relentlessly rise over time. To paraphrase most investment disclaimers, past results do not guarantee future success.

Remember the pizza delivery story – the activities and behaviors that helped Tony drive his brother out of business didn't help him against the new competitor.

What about our dieter who dropped the 10 pounds? What if she wants to lose another five? Food consumption and exercise still matter, but now, with the higher goal, merely counting calories or the number of minutes in the gym each week might not be enough. The Performance Drivers must change. Now she might need to focus on the amount of sugar or starchy carbs consumed, or the number of high-intensity cardio workouts, to lose the next five pounds.

The same thing applies in business. As you hit your goals for quality, productivity, or sales performance, you almost assuredly need to take performance to a higher level. The salesperson who is hitting her sales goals by building account plans and setting goals for each customer visit might need to target customers more effectively or focus on products with higher profit margin potential.

You Need to Redefine Your Performance Drivers Because the Goals Have Changed Due to a Change in Performance Requirements or Expanding Expectations

A disruptive competitor enters the market. Existing competitors introduce new products or services, or they cut prices. This may force you to set new or higher goals or even reposition your whole strategy. Whatever the cause, when your critical Result-Oriented Goals change, you must go back to step one and redefine your Performance Drivers.

Motorola faced a challenging pager market in the 1980s. Like many U.S. manufacturers, Motorola found itself falling behind foreign competitors on quality. To stay competitive, Motorola had to set the quality bar higher. The company moved from measuring quality performance in defects per 100 units to defects per million.

The change required a top-to-bottom revamping of Performance Drivers. Motorola leaders realized they needed to adopt tools like statistical process control. They invested heavily in training team members in the use of statistical process control techniques.

Today, on-line retailers are putting traditional brick and mortar retailers out of business. If they want to survive, the brick and mortar retailers must dramatically change what they are doing to provide a better customer experience than customers can get on-line.

Virtually every industry faces challenges from both existing competitors and others who seem to come from nowhere to disrupt their industries. It's critical to constantly re-evaluate your goals to ensure they are high enough to stay ahead of the competition, and then change the Performance Drivers to hit those higher levels of performance.

THOUGHT STARTER QUESTIONS

1. How well do you know which critical behaviors distinguish between high performers and average performers in your role?
2. What could you learn from others that might allow you to perform at a higher level?
3. How much time do you spend actively working on your Performance Drivers compared with other activities that aren't as crucial to hitting your goals?

4. How much time do your team members spend on their Performance Drivers versus other activities? What activities are imposed upon them by the organization that detracts from time better spent on critical activities?

5. How effectively do you track your Performance Drivers? What can you change to make the Performance Drivers more easily trackable or make your tracking system easier to use?

6. What aspects of performance could be, or need to be, taken to a higher level? And what could be taken to a higher level by identifying different Performance Drivers?

FIRST STEPS

1. Identify the Performance Drivers for one of your critical Result-Oriented Goals. Repeat with other critical goals.

2. Set up a tracking system for one or two of your Performance Drivers.
   - Is there an app that would be helpful?
   - Would it be easier and more time efficient to build a simple paper tracking system?
   - Track the Performance Drivers for at least a week or two.

3. Step back from the data and look for any correlation between your execution of the Performance Drivers and the results you achieve on your goals.

4. Identify the things that distract you from executing on your Performance Drivers (check all that apply):
   - Lack of clarity about what your goals or Performance Drivers ought to be.
   - Team members interrupting you with unrelated requests.
   - Your email inbox.
   - Too many different assignments or responsibilities competing for attention.
   - Having to respond to emergencies or "fire-fighting."
   - Dealing with inefficient processes or systems that slow your progress.
   - Other.

Now ask yourself:
- How can you avoid those distractions?
- If you can't avoid them, how can you best manage them?
- Then, when you're free from distraction, how can you get back on track with your Performance Drivers as quickly as possible?

BIBLIOGRAPHY

Ericsson, Anders and Pool, Robert. (2016) *Peak: Secrets from the New Science of Expertise.* New York, NY: Houghton Mifflin Harcourt.

Gladwell, Malcolm. (2008) *Outliers: The Story of Success.* New York, NY: Little, Brown and Company, Hachette Book Group.

Holiday, Ryan. (2014) *The Obstacle Is the Way: The Timeless Art of Turning Trials into Triumphs.* New York, NY: Penguin.

8

Follow-up/Follow-through: The Glue that Holds It All Together

Why don't team members complete tasks on time? Why do they complete some work, but with key parts missing? Why does it come as a surprise when they come up short at the moment of truth?

To answer these questions, you might ask yourself, "Why don't my kids clean their rooms after I've asked them hundreds of times?"

Imagine "clean up your room" as a strategic goal for your household. You **communicate**: You sit down and have a meeting with your daughter to discuss the critical importance of keeping her room clean. You talk about **success criteria**: What does a clean room look like, and how frequently does it need to stay that way to pass muster? You **create a SET goal**: The room will have all clothes in the hamper or drawers, no more than one to two toys will be out of the closet at any time, and the floors will be free of trash by her birthday. You provide an incentive: If she accomplishes the goal, you'll buy her a new bicycle. It seems to work. Your child wants that new bike, she understands what's expected, and she agrees she's more than capable of doing it.

You put this process in place and then ... nothing. Day in, day out, you go to work, your child goes to school, you both come home, eat dinner, and then your child goes off to bed.

For some reason, you never go upstairs to your child's room – maybe you brought home a lot of work or you've been catching up on your favorite television series. But no worries, you and your child have this

Strategy to Execution to Results thing DOWN! That room is sure to be spotless, right?

Er ... wrong.

Her birthday arrives, and her room looks like a tornado paid a recent visit. What happened? You outlined the strategy. You followed the process. Why didn't your kid execute?

This is the final element in the Strategy-Execution-Results (SXR) process, the one that provides the glue that holds the Seven Gear Framework together: Follow-up/Follow-through.

Granted, the stakes for cleaning a bedroom are pretty low. But are we any better about following up and following through at work? With so many things competing for your attention, it's easy to forget to circle back on the strategic goals you outlined last week, last month, or at the beginning of the year.

Does this sound familiar? While working with one organization, we were told about one manager who would assign tasks to her team, but never follow up.

Her team members learned to wait for the manager to ask a second time before starting work on a task. "I feel uncomfortable ignoring my boss," one of them said. "But we all do it, because we don't want to waste time on things that don't matter. I mean, if the boss doesn't care enough to follow up, why should I follow through?"

Often, she would never bring it up again.

In her book *Organized for Success*,[1] Stephanie Winston writes: "Failure to meet deadlines, honor commitments, monitor staff, return calls and keep track of long-term projects is the most underrated cause of chaos and failure in business life."

LACK OF FOLLOW-UP/FOLLOW-THROUGH WREAKS ORGANIZATIONAL CHAOS

During the heyday of the burgeoning market for PCs (yeah, way back in the early 1990s), we were working with a PC manufacturer in the United States. They had a decent market share (#4 or #5) in

[1] *Organized for Success*, Stephanie Wilson, Penguin Random House, 2004.

the United States, so at that point in time, they had a shot at being a significant player as the industry sorted itself out.

Unfortunately, they were killed by a lack of Follow-up/Follow-through. At that time, being first to market with the next generation of PCs – which occurred every 6–12 months – was considered to be the critical competitive advantage. First to market allowed companies to charge higher prices, and generate better margins, in the small windows in which there were few, if any, alternatives. Unfortunately, XYZ company was historically 2–3 months behind the faster players to the market.

Inside the organization, there was no accountability for hitting dates in project launch plans. Nor was there any diagnosis or learning around what caused the launch delays. Just an enormous amount of pressure to hit unrealistic launch dates. In fact, as we learned from several leaders, the only accountability was on *committing to* the project plan, no matter how unrealistic you thought it was. No one then held you accountable for actually hitting the dates, you just had to commit.

As a result, the company was late to the market for virtually every generation of PC. Because they did rush products into the marketplace, customers often faced quality and technical issues. XYZ tried to remedy those problems by hiring more customer service and technical support staff, which then drove their costs higher.

The combination of lower prices from being late to market and higher costs thinned out margins and eventually contributed to the organization's demise in the PC market.

Businesspeople generally understand this, and yet they still fall short. Mike Brunett, one of the excellent leaders in our manufacturing team when I was at Perrier, said it this way, "Follow-up/Follow-through is the most critical step in the process, and we stink at it!"

It's clear that although many people understand WHY Follow-up/Follow-through is important, they don't know HOW to do it.

Let's start with what effective Follow-up/Follow-through should look like. When done well, Follow-up/Follow-through:

- Shifts **responsibility** for both performance and accounting for that performance from the leaders to the performers.
- Generates **learning** about the overall execution effort.
- Creates **accountability** for delivering results.
- **Frees** up leaders' time that is otherwise spent tracking people down or wondering what the heck is going on.
- Provides a powerful platform for **effective coaching**.

Obviously, creating accountability is important. And, often, when we discuss Follow-up/Follow-through, that's where all the attention goes. But the focus on learning embedded in effective Follow-up/Follow-through is at least as important.

We start with this assumption: By and large, people come to work every day trying to do their best.

So, why does performance ever come up short? For dozens of reasons, most of which are addressed by the SXR Framework:

Maybe they are unclear on their goals, or the goals are poorly defined. Remember what happened when we played 5-on-5 in Chapter 5?

Maybe the performer doesn't have the capabilities necessary to effectively execute his Performance Drivers.

Or, as we discussed in Chapter 3, maybe there is misalignment in the architecture that punishes doing the right thing or rewards unproductive work.

Approaching Follow-up/Follow-through from a learning mindset allows those issues to bubble to the surface. If the objective of Follow-up/Follow-through is just to create accountability, then factors like those might be missed. We end up with the classic control-accountability mismatch: We're holding performers accountable for performance in which they are, at best, only partially in control of the outcomes.

THE WELLS FARGO MELTDOWN: A FAILURE OF LEADERSHIP (AND LEARNING!)

The Wells Fargo scandal was in large part a failure of "learning" from a consistent Follow-up/Follow-through process.

Wells Fargo fired more than 5,000 workers for creating millions of fake customer accounts, charging unwarranted mortgage fees, and pressuring customers to buy auto insurance they didn't need. The bad behavior was at least in part an effort to meet the unrealistic sales goals they operated under. But after the initial scandal, the bank continued to uncover problems. Workers were selling customers pet insurance and other products they didn't fully understand. They charged wealth-management and foreign exchange clients improper or excessive fees. A computer glitch caused hundreds of foreclosures. Each disclosure led to another round of refunds, bad publicity, and punishment. From Fall 2016 to the end of 2018, Well Fargo paid about $4 billion in settlements and fines. Wells Fargo's CEO departed.

"Wells Fargo is still trying to sweep up broken glass," William Klepper, a management professor at Columbia Business School, told CNN. "But they're finding it all over the place."

No one in the chain of command at Wells Fargo, from the CEO down to the supervisors who pressured sales and service associates, should get off the hook. As a group, they placed the goal of generating sales higher than serving their customers. As a group, they failed to learn how unrealistic sales goals encouraged a wide range of customer abuse.

It's well known within the banking industry that customers are more profitable when they have more products with a financial institution. So, it's not surprising that Wells Fargo, and many other banks, would set goals for account penetration, i.e., selling more products to each customer. Some Wells Fargo leaders at virtually every level of the organization held their team members ruthlessly accountable for selling products, even if it meant selling them to customers who didn't need or want them.

Had the focus been on learning...

- Which customers would benefit from buying additional products? Which ones won't? Why not?

- What, if anything, needs to change about the products we're selling to be more marketable?
- Which other customers might actually want these products?

...the whole disaster might have been avoided.

So, "learning" through the Follow-up/Follow-through process must come first, but...

Follow-up/Follow-through Must also Create Accountability

Some organizations abuse the idea of holding people accountable. For them, holding someone accountable means punishing people after something goes wrong, even if the problem was outside their control.

But, when there is no accountability, it means that performance, and/ or your values, don't matter. That is about the most disrespectful thing we can do to high performers. Left unchecked, it can create a downward spiral in performance. ... "If results don't matter, because that dude over there hasn't done a lick of work in months, then why should I bust my ass to perform?" Lack of accountability kills team member engagement.

Done well, though, Follow-up/Follow-through does more than creating accountability. It allows people to *be accountable* rather than *being held accountable* by their leaders. The difference is subtle but critical. In high engagement environments, people are responsible and accountable for their results. As one phenomenal leader we know says to all the new team members in his organization, "Own your results," which essentially means, "Be accountable; don't wait for someone to hold you accountable."

To create effective Follow-up/Follow-through:

- Leaders and performers mutually agree upon the Follow-up/Follow-through frequency or cycle time.
- Performers are responsible for scheduling the specific follow-up time on their manager's calendar – or short-circuiting the agreed-upon cycle if they hit a stumbling block.
- The performer is responsible for leading the conversation about what the goals are, what performance has looked like since the last Follow-up/Follow-through conversation, what caused any performance gaps and what the plan is moving forward to lift performance to a higher level or close any performance gaps.

When people follow this process, we rarely, if ever, hear this conversation:

"Yeah, my goal was to sell 100,000 units this month. I sold 50,000, but I have no clue why."
Or, "Yeah, I know I said I was going to do that in our last conversation, but I just chose not to do it."

Effective Follow-up/Follow-through consists of three main steps:

- Set the rhythm.
- Hold effective Follow-up/Follow-through conversations.
- Verify and document next steps.

SET THE RHYTHM

The first critical step in effective Follow-up/Follow-through is to set the rhythm – establishing a consistent timeframe for meeting, updating, and assessing progress toward the project's goal.

Once the rhythm has been established, the burden is on the *performer* to follow up with the leader at the agreed-upon time. Instead of having to nag performers about scheduling their next status meeting, leaders can focus their attention on their own critical goals and priorities.

How frequently should they meet? The answer is generally driven by the performer's needs and the nature of the goal or task.

The Performer's Needs

There are four factors to consider in determining the right rhythm for each performer. They include:

- The performer's current performance level.
- The performer's skills and ability to perform the task.
- The performer's level of engagement in performing the tasks necessary to achieve the goal.
- The performer's confidence in her ability to hit the goal.

Gauging the performer's current performance level means asking, "Is this person performing at or above target?" If so, that might suggest a slightly longer cycle. If not, she may need more frequent follow-up.

The second factor is the performer's skill level and ability to achieve his goals. Can this person hit his goals and execute his Performance Drivers when he applies himself to a task? Or does he struggle, no matter how hard he tries?

If you're dealing with the person who gets things done and who others go to when they hit roadblocks, then her Follow-up/Follow-through cycle can be longer. If you're dealing with an unproven person who might be a bit out of his depth, you might require a shorter cycle until he gets the hang of his job.

The third critical factor to consider when setting the Follow-up/Follow-through cycle is the team member's engagement in doing what's necessary to achieve goals and execute Performance Drivers.

It does not matter how much talent a person has if she lacks the motivation to execute. Understanding the cause of the commitment issue can help determine whether to shorten or lengthen the Follow-up/Follow-through cycle. We've seen both of these scenarios play out:

> When a leader over-manages the Follow-up/Follow-through cycle, the performer may feel: "Heck, my manager is just going to make all the decisions anyhow. Why should I commit myself to this?" The performer's objective essentially becomes to survive from one Follow-up/Follow-through cycle to the next. As one team member told us, "No one ever asks my boss a question because he will give you THE answer. It's hard to commit to a project when your boss always thinks he has a better answer regardless of how good the work you do."
>
> Or, the manager we described at the beginning of this chapter who never followed up on any assignment she gave her team. In that case, her team members were rarely engaged in the work because she under-managed the Follow-up/Follow-through process.

The last critical factor in understanding the performer's needs is her confidence in her ability to achieve the goals or execute the Performance Drivers. If she lacks confidence, it might be appropriate to shorten up the cycle time to enable the performer to generate some small wins or demonstrate progress. Counter-intuitively, it may occasionally also make sense to lengthen the Follow-up/Follow-through cycle to clearly communicate that the leader believes the performer has the capability to execute and achieve the goal.

By considering these four factors together, we can arrive at a rough idea of how frequent each performer's Follow-up/Follow-through cycle should be. Let's run a few common scenarios through this framework to see how it works.

FOLLOW-UP/FOLLOW-THROUGH CYCLES: WHAT'S "SHORTER" AND "LONGER?"

We purposely use the terms shorter and longer rather ambiguously. There is a little art, to go along with the science, of establishing the Follow-up/Follow-through rhythm.

In general, "longer" means at least weekly and, for most people means every two weeks, monthly, or even quarterly.

"Shorter" means weekly, daily, or even hourly. In the case of a new team member, or someone learning a really new skill, it can even mean "constantly" as the new person learns the new capability under the tutorship of another team member.

"Longer" NEVER means less frequently than quarterly – that's "abdication."

Finally, standing meetings, like daily pre-shift briefings or scrums in agile environments, or weekly or monthly meetings are often used effectively as parts of the Follow-up/Follow-through process.

The Rookie

Let's say you just hired a new team member who brings a ton of new capabilities, raw talent, and enthusiasm to the organization. However, he may not yet know how to apply those raw capabilities to his specific Result-Oriented Goals and Performance Drivers. So, the overall skill to actually do the job may be more moderate than his raw skills would suggest. What is his performance level? Since he's new on the job, his performance is likely below the standard we ultimately expect (Figure 8.1).

What about his confidence and commitment? Typically, the new team member or person in a new role will be highly committed. You wouldn't have hired him otherwise, right? Confidence can be a variable. He may be confident in his overall capabilities but wondering how he fits into the new

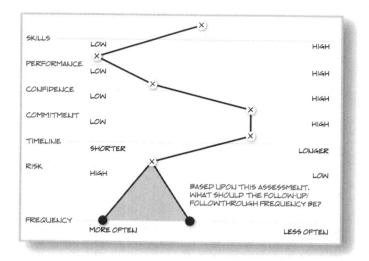

FIGURE 8.1
Follow-up/Follow-through for The Rookie.

role or with his new team. In such a case, the Follow-up/Follow-through cycle might be more frequent to give the leader an opportunity to celebrate small wins and progress.

In the first few days on the job, the Follow-up/Follow-through cycle might be daily or even every few hours. Or the new team member might be assigned to work side by side with a mentor, in which case the Follow-up/Follow-through cycle will be nearly continuous.

As the new team member demonstrates that he can operate safely and effectively on his own, you can gradually decrease the frequency of the Follow-up/Follow-through cycles.

Now, let's look at a performer with very different needs.

The Pro in Position

The Pro has been with the organization for several years. She is currently meeting or exceeding all her goals and is widely recognized as an expert in her role. She often trains and develops or mentors new team members. She's been doing the job at a high level, so we know her ability is high. And, she's highly confident and highly committed to the goal.

These factors indicate that the Follow-up/Follow-through cycle would be less frequent – maybe monthly or quarterly versus daily or weekly.

It's important to note, however, that even for The Pro, the cycle time is not forever. That would feel like abdication on the part of the leader, and even the best performers would begin to wonder if the goal and their performance matter (Figure 8.2).

Let's look at one more scenario:

When Performance Slips

In the case of rookies or pros, the Follow-up/Follow-through cycle is often obvious. Rookies, even high performing ones, usually benefit from shorter cycles, even if it's for nothing more than to ensure they're getting a feel for the organization's culture and values. Pros can operate on a much longer leash, but sometimes it can get complicated. You might, for example, encounter a team member who has performed well in the past but has slipped recently. See Figure 8.3.

Now he's performing below standard. You probably need to shorten his Follow-up/Follow-through cycle until you have a better understanding of what's behind the performance drop and a good reason to believe the performer has bounced back.

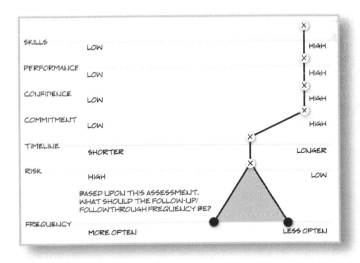

FIGURE 8.2
Follow-up/Follow-through for The Pro.

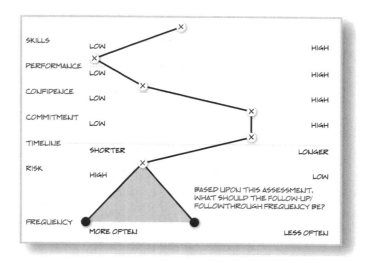

FIGURE 8.3
Follow-up/Follow-through when performance slips.

The Nature of the Goal or Task

The nature of the goal or task also impacts the Follow-up/Follow-through cycle. Here are three common issues:

- Whether the goal or task is a part of regular job responsibilities or a part of a project.
- The timeline for task or project completion.
- The level of risk – safety, customer, financial, operational, or other – from performers not achieving their goals.

Project work sometimes requires special attention. People on the project team might not be as familiar with their project tasks as their usual job responsibilities.

So, it might be appropriate to tighten up the Follow-up/Follow-through cycle. The key question is whether both the performer and the leader believe the performer has the skills and capabilities he needs to perform the task or achieve the goal.

Next, consider the timeline for the task or project completion. Generally, a closer deadline or project milestone would suggest shorter Follow-up/

Follow-through cycles that allow you to adjust quickly and troubleshoot problems.

Finally, we should consider the level of risk – safety, customer, financial, operational, or other. Higher risk would suggest a tighter rhythm. You're essentially buying insurance, sacrificing a bit of everyone's precious time to make absolutely sure the high-risk project is being executed properly. Shorter cycles help protect against the risk of a costly, or even life-threatening, failure.

Whatever the situation, the performer and leader should agree ahead of time on the timeframe to discuss performance and progress toward critical goals, results achieved and how the execution of the Performance Drivers impacted those results.

Leaders need to balance setting Follow-up/Follow-through cycles that are too tight – which can feel like micro-management – and cycles that are too loose – which can feel like abdication.

But if the consequences of failure are minor, then giving performers space to learn through trial and error is worth the downside. Failure is a great teacher, and you don't want to deny performers opportunities to learn by over-managing risk.

HOLDING EFFECTIVE FOLLOW-UP/FOLLOW-THROUGH CONVERSATIONS

A few years ago, we were talking to a coaching client of ours. He was a great leader with a bright future. When we got to the topic of Follow-up/Follow-through, he practically started yelling: "You know what frustrates me? When I ask people for updates on what they are working on and they launch into a long-winded, rambling diatribe shrouded in fog and ambiguity and leave me understanding less about the situation than when the conversation started."

It reminds us a lot of how our kids answer questions:

How was school today? "Fine."
What did you do? "Nothing."
What did you learn? "Nothing."

Or when the server or manager in a restaurant asks, "How was dinner?"
"Fine."

If we want better answers, we must ask better questions.

The 5×5 Follow-up/Follow-through Conversation

In response to our client's frustrations, we outlined five questions to cut
through the fog and allow leaders and performers to focus directly on
factors that are either driving or impeding success. Best of all, these five
questions can be answered in five minutes or less. We call this the 5×5
Conversation.

Depending on the answers, you can then decide where you might need
to dive in deeper.

1. *What are your Top 3 goals?*

   This question is a quick check, to make sure the leader and performer agree on what the performer's goals are. If there's a disconnect, then it might be necessary to take a little extra time to realign
   the performer's critical goals. In some cases, it's a matter of realigning attention and performance to the critical goals. In other cases,
   the learning may be about understanding why the performer is out
   of alignment. Is the leader or the organization somehow sending signals that something other than the performer's Top 3 goals is more
   important?

2. *What were the results during the last (week, month, quarter)?*

   This draws a direct line between the performer's goals and results,
   just like we discussed in Chapter 5 on SETting Results-Oriented
   Goals. If performance is at or above target, it can lead to a conversation about whether the goal is completed, and the performer should
   move on to the next critical goal, or if the goal could be adjusted to
   help them perform at an even *higher* level.

   If performance is below target, it leads to a discussion regarding
   the root causes of the performance gap, which we will discuss more
   in Question #4.

   Also, if the performer doesn't know where performance is relative
   to target, this can lead to a conversation around the scorecard and
   what must be done to make it more visible.

3. *What did you do during the last (week, month, quarter) relative to those goals?*

This question helps the performer and leader reflect on the extent to which the performer executed her Performance Drivers versus time spent on non-critical activities. This is the business equivalent of coaches and players grading game film and reminds the performer that, while leaders can guide and mentor, she is ultimately responsible for her own performance.

This also provides an opportunity for the leader and performer to discuss whether she has the skills and capabilities to effectively execute the Performance Drivers. If not, they can identify appropriate development opportunities to boost those capabilities.

4. *What caused any gaps?*

The performer's answer gives the leader a sense of how aware the performer is of any performance gaps. Meanwhile, self-diagnosis helps keep the responsibility for performance with the performer. If the performer can't effectively diagnose the cause, then the leader might have to step in to help him reflect more deeply on his performance and work through the issues.

During this part of the conversation, the leader and performer can recognize and discuss the extent to which performance gaps are caused by the performer (failure to focus on the Critical Goals or effectively execute his/her Performance Drivers) or by other factors. It's critical for people to own their results. If performers aren't thinking in terms of their goals and Performance Drivers, that lack of alignment may indicate that they are not owning their results. It's also important for leaders to recognize other barriers to performance and either knock them down or enable the performer to knock them down.

5. *What is your plan for the next (week, month, quarter)?*

The leader wants to learn if the performer has a plan that will keep performance on track or get performance back on track. In most cases, if the plan makes sense the leader will reinforce the plan and schedule the next Follow-up/Follow-through conversation.

If the plan doesn't make sense, this creates an opportunity to more deeply explore the performer's thinking. In some cases, it may be appropriate for the performer to experiment with his/her approach to getting performance on track. In other cases, it may require the leader to provide more direction and/or teach the performer a more effective way to resolve the gap.

> If this is a recurring performance issue that remains unresolved after multiple Follow-up/Follow-through cycles, or if the performer can't come up with a sensible plan, then the conversation might need to take a different direction. These are signs that the leader should get more deeply engaged in helping the performer identify and understand the causes of any gaps and build a plan that has a higher probability of success.

Taken together, these five magic questions help ensure execution stays on track with the goals.

The 5×5 Conversation Makes Leaders Better Coaches

The 5×5 Conversation allows leaders to focus their coaching efforts more directly on the places they need to coach. For instance, if the leader sees the performer is misaligned on her goals, the leader knows to coach there. If she is performing above goal or target, this provides an opportunity for the leader to challenge her to perform at an even higher level. On the other hand, if the performer is not acting on her key Performance Drivers, or executing them poorly, the 5×5 Conversation allows the leader and performer to zero in on that.

DOCUMENT AND VERIFY NEXT STEPS

The last part of an effective Follow-up/Follow-through process is to follow up the Follow-up!

First, you want to be absolutely clear about *who* is going to do *what* by *when*.

If performance is on track, this may be as simple as the leader and performer verifying when the next Follow-up/Follow-through discussion will take place. If performance is off-track for any reason, or if anything else is causing performance to be less than it ought to be, then it's critical to document *who* is going to act on *what*.

Does the performer need to engage in a development effort to improve his skills and capabilities? Does the leader need to help get the performer engaged in that opportunity? Does the leader need to take some action to eliminate friction or misalignment with any of the Seven Gears?

The very act of leaders following up and expecting performers to follow through sends a clear message that critical goals and Performance Drivers matter. The Follow-up/Follow-through process ensures that regular attention is paid to the critical goals, Visible Scorecards, and Performance Drivers that drive effective execution. Just as kids are more likely to do their homework or clean their rooms if a parent pays attention, performers in the workplace are more likely to perform if their leaders consistently pay attention to their performance. More importantly, the Follow-up/Follow-through process provides a critical learning opportunity for the performer, the leader, and the organization as a whole – if there is a gap in performance, the Follow-up/Follow-through process allows everyone to explore the causation and then identify appropriate solutions before performance or behavior gets too far off-track.

THOUGHT STARTER QUESTIONS

1. How consistently do you follow up on the performance in your organization?
2. How well do people in your organization "own their accountability?" How often are they held accountable for something they don't fully control?
3. How accountable are people for both performance and for playing within the values of your organization?
4. How effectively does the organization use any existing Follow-up/Follow-through processes to learn about which gears provide the greatest opportunity to connect Strategy-to-Results?
5. What, if anything, drives the Follow-up/Follow-through cycle? What should change to ensure Follow-up/Follow-through is more consistent and effective?

FIRST STEPS

1. Identify an accountability partner to work through SXR with. Set your joint Follow-up/Follow-through cycle to ensure both of you stay on track with your efforts to better connect Strategy-to-Results.
2. Establish a Follow-up/Follow-through rhythm with each of your team members and/or your manager. Base it upon the performer's needs for guidance and support. Start slowly at first. Work with one person. Then expand as you get more practice and experience with setting the cycle and following up.
3. Begin utilizing the 5×5 Conversation to make your Follow-up/Follow-through conversations both more effective and more efficient.
4. Develop a team meeting follow-up list: Outline who committed to what, what they accomplished, and where there might be gaps. Review the list at the beginning and end of each team meeting to keep track of what was accomplished and identify any unclosed loops.

BIBLIOGRAPHY

Blanchard, Kenneth, Zigarmi, Patricia & Zigarmi, Drea. (1985) *Leadership and the One Minute Manager*. New York, NY: William Morrow and Company, Inc.

Tate, Rick & White, Julie. (2012) *Performance Coaching for Business Results: Common Traps and Opportunities*. E-book: http://www.impactachievement.com

Winston, Stephanie. (2004) *Organized for Success: Top Executives and CEOs Reveal the Organizing Principles That Helped Them Reach the Top*. New York, NY: Crown Business.

9

Time to eXecute! Aligning the Gears to Drive Better Results

A few years ago, a friend of mine opened a regional sales office in Mexico for his US-based company. While he was looking for a location for the new office, his leader, the Vice President (VP) of Sales for the company, visited. The sales manager asked his boss, "What do you think we ought to do?" His VP responded, "I guess we ought to go sell something." And they did.

Now that you've reached the end of this book and the beginning of your journey with Strategy-Execution-Results (SXR), you might be asking the same question as the sales manager. To paraphrase him, I'd suggest we ought to go "execute something."

How's that for precise guidance? There's a serious point behind my vague answer: Choosing to take the first step is more important than pouring over your organization for weeks to pick the absolute best starting point.

This chapter will help you think through how to get started. Driving forward on the SXR process, whether it's for yourself, your team, or your whole organization, is just a microcosm of what we've covered in this book:

- Define the Gap: Identify what most needs to be fixed.
- SET Goals: What are the two or three things you want to accomplish to close the gap, and when will you achieve them?
- Build a Scorecard: How will you track progress in closing the gap(s) you identified?
- Define Your Performance Drivers: What must you DO to execute your plan?
- Create a Follow-up/Follow-through Process: Identify a partner who can help you learn and create accountability to execute your plan.

We can only guess at what will allow you to improve the most in the shortest amount of time, but remember: Don't let visions of near-miraculous transformation intimidate you into doing nothing. Take the first step. Here's what I mean:

In a perfect world, you could simultaneously work on, align, and optimize all seven gears. Strategy drives ideal results when all seven gears are aligned and working together, but you also can improve by fixing any single gear.

Some gears take longer to improve than others. If your team's goals aren't aligned to your organization's strategy, you can make real progress on Setting Result-Oriented Goals within days. On the other hand, if your organization's values and culture are not aligned to your overall purpose, mission, and strategy, that one takes a while to clean up.

So, which gear will boost results the most for your organization, your team, or yourself? Which orange will squeeze out the most juice?

To find the answer, you might ask:

- Which gear is the wobbliest? (Sorry, had to use a very technical term!)
- Which gear provides an opportunity for the quickest win? (Hint: It's often SETting Result-Oriented Goals aligned to the strategy.)
- Which gear do I have the most influence over? What's the timeframe for taking action, and then seeing results?

Actions which typically take longer (but have larger organization-wide impact):

- Align the culture to the strategy.
- Change succession planning and talent management processes to ensure you're placing the Right People in the Right Roles with the Right Capabilities.
- Change systems, structures, and processes to align with the strategy.

Actions which typically take less time to enact (but may have more narrowly focused results):

- Align individual and/or team goals to the strategy.
- Build Visible Scorecards at the team and/or individual level.
- Identify the critical Performance Drivers and align individual and team performance to them.
- Implement a new, more rigorous Follow-up/Follow-through process.

Actions you must do regardless because they set the foundation for success:

- Build a culture aligned with your strategy that enables everyone to perform at their best.
- Attract, retain, and develop the talent that enables success.
- Improve your communications up, down, and sideways to engage everyone in the effort to translate Strategy-to-Results.

You must assess *your* situation – what most needs work and what you can have the most influence over – and then prioritize the actions you'll take. If you'd like some help, I'm inviting you to send me a question. I'll show you how at the end of this book.

Let's try some hypothetical cases:

A frontline supervisor plays 5-on-5 with his team. He finds that on average only 2 out of 5 goals match. He doesn't have a lot of influence over who gets hired into his organization, although he does occasionally conduct interviews of potential new hires. As he works to align the goals for each team member to the strategy of his organization, he also finds out that several of his team members do not have the skills and capabilities to execute their Performance Drivers at the highest level.

So, which gear should he focus on? His primary focus should be on SETting Result-Oriented Goals with each team member. Through SET goals, he can concentrate on building the capabilities of his team members, so he has – within his influence – the Right People in the Right Roles with the Right Capabilities.

A senior executive in the same organization also sees that frontline team members and supervisors don't have the same goals. She's not in the best position to play 5-on-5, separated by distance and organizational layers from the frontline teammates. But she's in a better position than the frontline supervisor to do something about getting the right people into the organization (Right, Right, Right, from a different perspective). So, she focuses on changing the company's compensation system, which is still rewarding behavior consistent with the company's former strategy. Once that is fixed, the company will be more attractive to the kind of people necessary to execute its new strategy.

Table 9.1 summarizes some general observations about who, at different levels, tends to have the most ability to fix components of the Seven Gears.

TABLE 9.1

What's My Play?

Gear	Frontline Leader	Mid-Manager	Senior Exec, C-Suite
Right, Right, Right	Develop the people you have. Ensure you have the people on your team playing the role that generates the best results while helping team members grow and develop.	Build and execute hiring practices that attract the right people into the right roles. Ensure people have access to the tools and resources they need to be successful. Be a steward of the values.	Shape the values of the organization to align with the strategy; be a steward of the values. Focus on building your "employment" brand that links to your overall branding strategy and allows you to attract and retain the talent you need. (You are amid a massive war for talent. Are you winning or losing?) Ensure the organization has a talent management process that lets you evaluate your bench strength, ensures a steady flow of talent, and helps you build the capabilities of your team.
Align the Architecture	Know what drives each of your team members. Help each one connect the organization's architecture – for example, recognition and rewards – to their interests.	Be vigilant about the effects of any misalignment in architecture; lead the effort to change systems, structures, and processes that are misaligned to the strategy. Best position in the organization to see how processes align to the strategy. Be a zealot about aligning them to the right results.	Remember you're the ultimate steward of the architecture, but not always the architect! Constantly ask whether you've got the architecture aligned to your strategy. Build strong, consistent values that provide stability and predictability while enabling systems, structures, and processes to evolve as necessary.

(Continued)

TABLE 9.1 (*Continued*)

What's My Play?

Gear	Frontline Leader	Mid-Manager	Senior Exec, C-Suite
Culture of Communications	Connect with your team. Build the foundational relationships of trust and respect that allow communications to flourish. Give more and better feedback. HOLD courageous conversations with your team and with your leaders. If you don't identify the obstacles to your team's success, your team members certainly aren't going to hear it from anyone else.	Don't be the Marshmallow! Connect with empathy; hear what people are really trying to communicate to you. Build environments founded on trust and respect in which people can hold the courageous conversations. Practice two up/two down communications. HOLD the courageous conversations.	Build environments founded on trust and respect in which people can hold the courageous conversations. Strive to create environments in which anyone in the organization can contact you directly … and it's okay. HOLD the courageous conversations.
SET Result-Oriented Goals	Play 5-on-5. Ensure goals are focused on results, not activities, wherever possible.	Play 5-on-5. Ensure the goals within your organization align with the overall organization's strategy.	Play 5-on-5. (Yeah, you too … we're amazed at the infrequency with which C-level executives hold conversations with each other about their top priorities.) Identify one or two areas in which your organization needs stretch goals and set them. Then, support the effort to change the organization to allow it to achieve the goal. When wandering the organization, routinely ask team members about the three to five critical goals and how they connect to the organization's strategy. Seek to understand the causation of any gaps you find.

(Continued)

TABLE 9.1 (*Continued*)

What's My Play?

Gear	Frontline Leader	Mid-Manager	Senior Exec, C-Suite
Visible Scorecard	Focus your attention on what matters; your team is watching. Ensure every individual and/or team has a Visible Scorecard that allows them to change the outcome of the game while it's being played. Use data for learning, not punishment.	Translate the organizational scorecard into goals for your division or department; ensure alignment up and down. What do you want to measure that you can't measure today? Be on a perpetual search for ways to simply measure the critical components of performance.	Establish the top-level scorecard that represents your strategy. Ensure the scorecard cascades to every level of the organization.
Performance Drivers	Help your team identify its critical Performance Drivers. Coach people up. Ensure your team members track their most critical Performance Drivers to instill more consistent execution AND provide early warning systems of performance gaps.	Connect your direct reports to best practices across the organization. Don't settle: Good enough is not good enough. Be on a constant search for best practices inside or outside your organization that allow you to lift performance.	At the strategic level, identify those activities that allow your organization to create competitive advantage. STOP doing those things that do not create value.

(*Continued*)

TABLE 9.1 (Continued)

What's My Play?

Gear	Frontline Leader	Mid-Manager	Senior Exec, C-Suite
Follow-up/ Follow-through	Work with your team members to change the Performance Drivers to lift performance when required. Utilize the principles of Purposeful and Deliberate Practice to improve the performance capabilities of the people on your team. Establish the appropriate Follow-up rhythm with each of your direct reports and/or your team. Utilize the Five-Question/Five-Minute Conversation to gauge overall results. Use it as the basis for coaching. Generate learning. Use the Five-Question Conversation as the starting point for root cause analysis on performance gaps. Be courageous … create accountability, when necessary.	Ensure your direct reports have regular Follow-up/Follow-through cycles set with their team members. Review what they review. How effectively are they using the Follow-up/Follow-through process as the basis for coaching, learning, and accountability?	Establish the rhythm for overall organizational Follow-up/Follow-through. Set the tone – generate learning first; create accountability second… …but *do* create accountability. Performance and playing within the value set must matter.

So, you've assessed. You've identified at least one or two gears that need better alignment or that could operate better. (You *have* identified something, right? Otherwise, you're suggesting you're in that awesome 10% of organizations that is effectively translating Strategy-to-Results ... at least for today!)

As you get ready to align and tune the gears you've identified need work, a few closing thoughts...

GET COMFORTABLE WITH BEING UNCOMFORTABLE

As with most efforts to improve existing capabilities or develop new ones, implementing SXR will likely seem hard at first. It's like quitting smoking, changing your eating habits, correcting your golf swing, or starting a new exercise routine. This is going to be uncomfortable.

Remember the story in Chapter 7 about correcting my golf swing. When I first started working with the golf pro, I was very comfortable standing over the ball ... and hit crappy shots in about a 270° arc around the tee box. Within ten minutes of assessing and then changing everything about my swing, I was completely uncomfortable. I felt like I was going to fall over merely standing over the ball. Yet, my swing and the results improved dramatically.

As you put SXR to work, you will likely feel a similar level of discomfort as you build the habits necessary to stay focused and execute both daily and over the longer term. It just takes some time, combined with a few slices and hooks along the way, to build new habits and new capabilities for yourself and within your organization.

You are essentially trading short-term discomfort of embedding new habits for long-term improvement in performance within your organization. Eventually, you will get to a new state in which translating SXR is second nature.

STEADFAST FOCUS/NIMBLE METHODS

Lao Tzu, the ancient China philosopher and apparently one of the world's first management consultants, said, "The journey of a thousand miles begins with one step."

We like to say that change, whether individual or across vast organizations, is a journey of 10,000 steps. The smartest people on earth can maybe figure out the first five or ten steps. The problem is that once you start taking the first two or three steps, the next 9,997 all change. That doesn't mean your first step was wrong. It does mean that the process of change is often unpredictable. You don't know what works or doesn't work. You can't always predict how others around you will react.

Remember what we talked about at the beginning of this book – *we operate in a world of perpetual whitewater.* The outside world is unpredictable and filled with swirling currents, rapids, and unseen drops. But, heck, that's the fun.

Back in the day – when I earned a college degree while spending much of my time paddling rivers in Georgia, North Carolina, and South Carolina, and occasionally attending class – our rallying cry was, "We aren't having any fun unless we feel like we're about to die." While you don't have to get that close to the edge, this journey will offer its own twists and turns.

Maintaining Steadfast Focus is critical. You must stay focused on the strategy you're trying to execute to create a competitive advantage even as you must apply nimble methods to adapt to constantly changing conditions.

FIND A LEARNING/ACCOUNTABILITY PARTNER

Finally, one of the best practices for driving SXR is to find a partner who will help you learn and hold you accountable. Engaging a learning/accountability partner will dramatically improve the quality and speed with which you implement the SXR Framework for yourself, your team, or your organization. Your partner will help you build and execute your own execution plan:

- SET Result-Oriented Goals.
- Build your Visible Scorecard.
- Identify Performance Drivers (what you will DO to execute your plan).
- Establish a Follow-up/Follow-through Process.

Finally, check out several tools that can help on our website at www.wwici.com.

They will help you assess where you're at, which gears you might want to focus attention on, and provide additional thoughts about how to drive forward. In addition, you can post success stories, challenges, and questions to the growing SXR community so that we can all learn from each other. We can all get better at driving SXR.

Congratulations on your decision to join the growing number of people, leaders, and organizations that want to align the Seven Gears and achieve truly outstanding results!

BIBLIOGRAPHY

The journey of a thousand miles begins with one step. Generally attributed to Lao Tzu, Tao Te Ching, between 4th and 6th century BC.

YOU'VE GOT IT IN GEAR, NOW

Stay in Gear

Become a Gearhead! Join the Strategy-Execution-Results Community

We live in a dynamic global environment. While
the principles embedded in SXR are timeless, their
application and best practices change over time.

To stay connected and learn from the best of what others are doing
drive over to the *Get in Gear: The Seven Gears that Drive Strategy
to Results* online community. For continuously updated content,
videos, MP3s, case studies, discussion forums, and more go to:

www.wwici.com/Gearheads

and enter the passphrase:

get results

Bibliography

Aileron (November 30, 2011) 10 Reasons Why Strategic Plans Fail. Forbes.

Hrebiniak, Lawrence G. (2013) *Making Strategy Work: Leading Effective Execution and Change.* Upper Saddle River, NJ: FT Press.

Knowledge@Wharton (August 10, 2005) Three Reasons Why Good Strategies Fail: Execution, Execution....

McGregor, Douglas. (1958) *The Human Side of Enterprise.* New York, NY: McGraw Hill.

McNeilly, Mark. (February 14, 2014) How to Avoid a "Strategy Fail. Fast Company.

Vermeulen, Freek. (November 8, 2017) Many Strategies Fail Because They're Not Actually Strategies. Harvard Business Review Digital Article.

Index

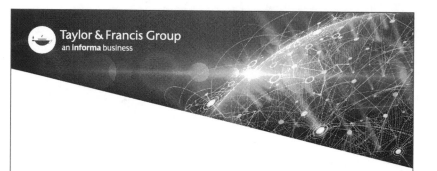